Play Up and Play the Game

PATRICK HOWARTH

Play Up
and
Play the Game

THE HEROES
OF POPULAR FICTION

EYRE METHUEN
LONDON

First published 1973
Copyright © 1973 Patrick Howarth
Printed in Great Britain for
Eyre Methuen Ltd
11 New Fetter Lane, EC4P 4EE
by Redwood Press Ltd, Trowbridge, Wiltshire

SBN 413 26110 7

Contents

Acknowledgements

Acknowledgements and thanks are due to the following authors, publishers and agents for the use of copyright material:
To Mrs Bambridge and the Macmillan Companies for extracts from *Stalky and Co.* by Rudyard Kipling;
To Hodder and Stoughton Ltd for extracts from *The Million Pound Deposit* by E. Phillips Oppenheim;
To John Murray (Publishers) Ltd for extracts from *The Four Feathers* by A.E.W. Mason, and *The Wages of Virtue* by P. C. Wren;
To Peter Newbolt and A. P. Watt and Son for the poem *Vitai Lampada* by Sir Henry Newbolt;
To Mrs Orczy-Barstow and A. P. Watt and Son for extracts from *The Scarlet Pimpernel* by Baroness Orczy (Hodder and Stoughton).

Play Up and Play the Game

There's a breathless hush in the Close tonight —
Ten to make and the match to win —
A bumping pitch and a blinding light,
An hour to play and the last man in.
And it's not for the sake of a ribboned coat,
Or the selfish hope of a season's fame,
But his Captain's hand on his shoulder smote —
'Play up! play up! and play the game!'

The sand of the desert is sodden red, —
Red with the wreck of a square that broke; —
The Gatling's jammed and the Colonel dead,
And the regiment blind with dust and smoke.
The river of death has brimmed his banks,
And England's far, and Honour a name,
But the voice of a schoolboy rallies the ranks:
'Play up! play up! and play the game!'

This is the word that year by year,
While in her place the School is set,
Every one of her sons must hear,
And none that hears it dare forget.
This they all with a joyful mind
Bear through life like a torch in flame,
And falling fling to the host behind —
'Play up! play up! and play the game!'

SIR HENRY NEWBOLT: *Vitai Lampada*

Introduction — The Nature of Newbolt Man

Sir Henry Newbolt visited Canada in 1923. There he was impressed by the old Scottish families, whom he described as providing the backbone of the country, 'and a jolly fine backbone it is too'. He considered they had an abundance of religion ('a good plain brand'), of morals, philosophy and business capacity. He found evidence too of a 'desire' for a great national art and poetry, and he was understandably gratified by the popular response to his own verses. 'As for "Play up and play the Game",' he wrote, 'it's a kind of Frankenstein monster that I created thirty years ago and now I find it falling on my neck at every street corner! In vain do I explain what is poetry: they roar for "Play up"; they put it on their flags and on their war memorials and their tombstones; it's their National Anthem.'

The exaggeration was slight enough to be permissible. Through nearly all his working life Newbolt was familiar with such popular acclaim. When he came to write his memoirs, *My World as in My Time,* he found no need, and probably had no inclination, to boost his reputation or to defend any of his actions. He was aware of the esteem he had enjoyed from the day he had begun to publish poetry, and his literary career was one of almost uninterrupted success.

1

Newbolt's first volume of poems was published in 1897, when he was aged thirty-five. Twenty-one editions appeared, and soon after the publication of the first he had almost daily enquiries from editors who wanted poems from him. When Newbolt was sixty-five the Bilston Urban District Council decided to celebrate the centenary of the laying of the foundation stone of St Mary's church in Bilston, where Newbolt's father had preached, by placing a tablet on the vicarage stating that Henry Newbolt had been born there in 1862. The number of those whose fame is such that local authorities erect memorial tablets to them in their lifetime cannot be large.

Newbolt was respected as a poet by some of the most eminent men in British public life, and with a number of them he was on friendly terms. He would dine alone with Sir Edward Grey and talk about birds. 'I wonder,' Newbolt commented, 'what he talks to other people about while the servants are in the room.' One of his books of verse was dedicated to Grey, whose wife, when expressing her pleasure at the compliment, wrote: 'He shall read "Hope the Hornblower" when he feels despondent.' When Harry Greene sang Newbolt's *Farewell* to Sir Charles Stanford's setting at a concert in the Albert Hall in December 1917, A. J. Balfour was reported to have laid down the sheet containing the words 'with a kind of sigh'. He then read a passage from Ecclesiasticus and on his way back to his seat said to Newbolt: 'That was a beautiful poem of yours, a most beautiful poem.' Newbolt mentioned the music, to which Balfour replied: 'I liked the poem much better than the music.'

Such feelings of respect and admiration were expressed too by writers of lasting distinction, poets among them. Robert Bridges, on first reading *Drake's Drum*

(Drake, he's in his hammock an' a thousand mile away,
Capten, art tha sleepin' there below?)

said in Newbolt's presence:

'It isn't given to a man to write anything better than that. I wish I had ever written anything half so good.' When Newbolt published a historical novel, *The New June,* H. G. Wells described the first part of it as being 'on the level of couldn't possibly be better'. Gertrude Bell took a similar view of another of Newbolt's now unread novels, *The Old Country,* declaring that he enjoyed an unfair advantage over the rest of mankind as a poet with a novelist's talent.

In the 1922 New Year Honours Newbolt was made a Companion of Honour. He received honorary degrees from the universities of Bristol, Glasgow, St Andrews, Sheffield, Toronto, Oxford and Cambridge. He was appointed editor of the *Monthly Review* in 1900. Although he had had no training as a historian and had never been a naval officer, he wrote two of the five volumes on naval operations in the official history of the war of 1914-18. During the same war he was invited, together with Lords Cromer, Haldane and Milner, to make a major contribution to a work on post-war reconstruction, his subject being patriotism.

Of all these distinctions and all this acclaim it can be said that they stemmed wholly from the publication of a relatively small number of poems, of which the one whose stanzas end 'Play up! play up! and play the game!' was fairly representative.

In the 1970s this is a puzzling phenomenon. Already in the 1930s, when I was a schoolboy, Newbolt's verses had become a subject of ridicule among the sophisticated young and even the not very young. Early in the 1970s I asked a group of intelligent and fairly well-read young people, who had just graduated from Cambridge University and who had all taken arts courses, what the name of Sir Henry Newbolt meant to them. The answer was in effect nothing. How then can the phenomenon be explained? Is it attributable primarily to changes in ethical codes or to changes in literary fashions? The answer must, of course, lie to a large extent in a subjective judgment of whether Newbolt did or did not have the quality of a true poet.

Newbolt had a facility for rhyme and a feeling for the compulsion and urgency of rhythm as well as for exotic place-names.

> He did not hear the monotonous roar that fills
> The ravine where the Yassin river sullenly flows;
> He did not see the starlight on the Laspur hills
> Or the far Afghan snows.

These can be valuable assets in a song-writer, and if he can find a composer to match his mood and his quality, a writer with such gifts may well produce something of lasting appeal. In this respect Newbolt was fortunate. Sir Charles Stanford, to whose settings Newbolt's songs were repeatedly sung on concert platforms, in seaside pavilions and in village halls, was a versatile and prolific composer to whom sea songs made a natural appeal. Perhaps the happiest example of the collaboration between the two men was in their joint creation of *The Old Superb:*

> So Westward ho! for Trinidad and Eastward ho! for Spain.

Newbolt wrote the words, as he put it, 'all in one piece', and the next morning Stanford completed the setting. In describing how this happened Newbolt wrote: 'Could one enjoy life more gloriously?'

Skill as a writer of what, in the phraseology of popular music, are known today as lyrics, must surely be accorded to Newbolt, but only an unusually generous modern critic would be likely to grant him much else. Banality is perhaps the most pervasive quality in his verse, banality of the kind found in the lines:

> There lay the enemy's ships, and sink or swim
> The flag was flying, and he was head of the line.

Cliché poetic terms of the kind which are copied and not felt —'fain', 'nigh', 'craven', 'sloth' —abound. For a man born in Staffordshire his preoccupation with Devon seems to stem not so much from a study of Elizabethan history as from the convenience of its rhyming with 'heaven'. The rhythms, too, soon become oppressive, and the latter-day reader, on encountering such lines as

There'll be many grim and gory,
There'll be few to tell the story,
But we'll all be one in glory,

must feel an almost irresistible urge to add 'when she comes'.

When Newbolt strayed outside his normal poetic field and went so far as to introduce the figure of a girl, the result, in *A Lady of Tender Age,* is no better than unconscious Shakespearean parody:

Ladies, life is a changing measure,
Youth is a lilt that endeth soon.

In all Newbolt's works I have been unable to find a line which seems to me true poetry, and if indeed his artistic poverty was as complete as it now appears to have been, the secret of his success, with the critical and the distinguished as well as with a wider public, must surely lie in his message. It is therefore primarily by his message that his importance in his lifetime should be judged.

Throughout his life Newbolt was a conformist, and his background and upbringing were conducive to the acceptance of those beliefs whose expression brought him fame and the acclaim of his contemporaries. His paternal grandfather had been a naval officer. His father, the Staffordshire clergyman, lectured on poetry, and Newbolt himself found his principal sources of escape as a boy from what he termed 'the tedium of a Midland town' in Latin and English poetry. The Latin classics were his principal academic discipline, a number of his poems were given Latin titles, and he exhibited a quiet pride in being able to record that H. G. Wells envied him his ability to decipher the Latin inscriptions on tombstones.

Schools not surprisingly played a major part in instilling in him the code which he comprehensively accepted. Of Hundon, the preparatory school he attended at Caistor in Lincolnshire, he wrote: 'The Hundon code, which made us fight our schoolboy battles, was a law against heathendom—the law that you cannot stand by while the weak are bullied by the strong, or accept an unjust indignity without resistance.' This law drove him into a fight with his best friend, who later became a general with a distinguished war record. But it was Clifton school, that forcing ground of professional soldiers, which left him with the most indelible and inspiring memories. His first sight of the school close was one which he never forgot, and he recorded it later in a story, in which he wrote of 'a wide green sward, level as a lawn, flooded in low sunlight, and covered in every direction with a multitude of white figures, standing, running, walking, bowling, throwing, batting—in every attitude that can express the energy and expectancy of youth.'

From the description of the scenes he passed to a consideration of 'the finely planned order and long–descended discipline they symbolized'. Sir Arthur Quiller-Couch wrote to Newbolt about these passages: 'Was it you or I, who heard the crack of bat on ball and caught his breath at first sight of the Close? It was, I, Sir, and here I catch you a–hugging one of my best memories.'

It was Clifton chapel which inspired the lines:

To set the cause above renown,
To love the game beyond the prize,
The foe that comes with fearless eyes . . .
To honour, while you strike him down,
Today and here the fight's begun,
Of the great fellowship you're free;
Henceforth the School and you are one,
And what You are, the race shall be.

'It's a pure marvel, a School,' Newbolt once wrote, 'and the intangible thing we call "House–feeling" is about the most wonderful thing in it.'

Newbolt admired to the point of reverence his headmaster at Clifton, Dr John Percival, and predictably he paid him the supreme compliment of describing him as being in the tradition of Arnold of Rugby. This tradition, he wrote, 'derived originally from the patriotism or public spirit of the Jew, the Greek and the Roman'. The Jews to whom he referred were almost certainly the warring Jews of the Old Testament, and the Romans quite certainly those of the years of the republic, for it is unlikely that Newbolt, even as a classical scholar, learnt much about the Roman empire other than the reiterated statement that it declined and fell. To Newbolt Percival was 'the most satisfying figure of a great man that could be felt or imagined'. His own last years at Clifton were, in his words, 'a currency of high purchasing power in terms of happiness', and when he went up to Oxford in the hope and belief that it would be a second Clifton, with opportunities, contests and pleasures magnified, he was understandably disappointed. 'I found,' he wrote, 'that there were differences, even defects.' If Newbolt was aware of any defects in the system or practices of his public school he did not record them.

It was at Clifton that Newbolt first formed his friendship with the future Field–Marshal Earl Haig. Unlike Newbolt, who was head of the school, Haig was academically undistinguished, possibly a little backward. Newbolt kindly used the phrase 'never high in the school lists', and contrasted this with Haig's qualities of character and solid athletic merit. More than fifty years after leaving school Newbolt, who had been a non–combatant in the war of 1914–18 because of his age, wrote in a letter:

> When I looked into Douglas Haig I saw what is really great —perfect acceptance, which means perfect faith. Owen and the rest of the broken men rail at the Old Men who sent the young to die: they have suffered cruelly, but in the nerves and not the heart—they haven't the experience or the imagination to know the extreme human agony —"Who giveth me to die for thee, Absalom, my son." Paternity apart, what Englishman of fifty wouldn't rather stop the shot himself than see the boys do it for them? I don't think these shell–shocked war poems will move our grandchildren greatly.

In my reading of Newbolt's works this is the nearest approach to an unkind comment I have come across, and the choice of target is significant. Nor is it surprising to find Newbolt, about the same time, not only lamenting the loss of Rupert Brooke but deploring the new tendency to label him 'patriotic' and classify him as second-rate.

Among Newbolt's other school friends was one whose later career was in effect an active expression of many of Newbolt's own ideals. This was Francis Younghusband, soldier, explorer and devout Christian, who travelled extensively in Manchuria and Afghanistan, was believed to have been the first European to cross the Gobi desert, and was the guiding spirit in the revival of attempts to climb Mount Everest. Younghusband once wrote to Newbolt:

> The greatest question which lies before us at present is the Chinese question, and the solution of that depends on the use we make of India and our genius for leading Asiatics. . . . If we can, besides looking after our own particular rights and interests, draw up with us to a higher level these hundreds of millions dependent on us, we shall have done a nobler work in the world than has been accomplished by any nation yet.

Their friendship was confirmed through an activity which had a natural appeal to both of them—cross-country running. A seven-mile race was held at Clifton known as the Short Penpole, and when they last competed in it at school Younghusband led Newbolt by only a yard until the final run-in, when Younghusband forged ahead to win. With considerable satisfaction Newbolt was able to record subsequently: 'I got my own back in a later year, when we both ran in the Old Cliftonians' race.' Old Cliftonians' race! No wonder Wells, who did not go to a public school, and Newbolt differed over the issue of what Wells called petty loyalties. Newbolt's reply to Wells's charge was that loyalty is a quality, not a quantity, and cannot be petty.

The loyalty to a school or schools which Newbolt felt with such intensity and expressed with such vigour was complemented by other group or institutional loyalties, the most compelling of which was the loyalty owed to the mother-country. On coming down from Oxford Newbolt followed the example, no doubt unconsciously, of another writer who had found inspiration in an almost mystic concept of a public school, Thomas Hughes, in reading for the Bar while being rather more interested in the voluntary work he did in a boys' club. Newbolt's club was in the Notting Hill area of London. This, he declared, gave him something he had always been looking for—some might say he wanted to see perpetuated—'the sense of corporate life'. The boys of Notting Hill, Newbolt wrote, 'enlarged my sense of patriotism and when I had to leave them I found nothing to replace them'.

What in fact did replace them was Newbolt's own writing in prose and in verse about England and the English. The title given to one of his books of poems was *The Island Race.* The stanzas of the title poem all end:

The sweep and splendour of England's war.

Another poem in the same book, *The Vigil,* opens with the lines:

England! where the sacred flame
Burns before the inmost shrine.

The stanza end-line here is:

Pray that God defend the right.

Yet it is in one of his prose works, a novel entitled *The Old Country,* that Newbolt's passionate, uncritical love for the concept of England, a largely mystical concept, is expressed most forthrightly. (To Newbolt, as to others of his generation, the concept of Britain was not particularly inspiring.)

'I love this Country,' Audrey said, 'I love it as I love nothing else in life. It is to me everything that men have ever loved—a mother, a nurse, a queen, a lover, and something greater and more sacred still. There is not one look of it that I shall ever forget or cease to long for, and I would as soon kill a friend as change the name of the smallest of its fields.'

'I understand,' he said, 'but I had almost forgotten that patriotism could be so intense and yet so local.'

'If you forget that,' she replied, 'you forget all.'

The mystical blends readily, all too readily perhaps, with the practical, and the superiority in action of the English over those nations whom they rule is not simply accepted but explicitly stated. *A Ballad of John Nicholson* has as its subject the disturbances and outrages of 1857 which became known through English history books as the Indian Mutiny. In the poem the principal antagonists are Mehtab Singh, described as 'proud and sly', and the Englishman with the conveniently homely name of John Nicholson. Mehtab Singh says of the English:

They have ruled us for a hundred years,
In truth I know not how.

Nicholson promptly provides the answer:

Have ye served us for a hundred years
And yet ye know not why?
We brook no doubt of our mastery,
We rule until we die.

Mehtab Singh and the other 'captains' duly capitulate with the comment: 'When the strong command obedience is best.'

Much of this is rather startling to modern susceptibilities and may not seem easily reconcilable with W. B. Yeats's statement that Newbolt's patriotism was 'the fine sort—patriotism that lays burdens upon a man, and not the patriotism that takes burdens off'. The reconciliation may be sought—whether it is to be found must be a matter of opinion—in the acceptance of service underlying many of Newbolt's utterances about England. Writing about the war of 1914-18, Newbolt made the point that his own generation when young had had 'neither cruel experiences nor dark apprehensions' to weaken them. They felt as heroes and heroines in a great saga. For them 'the great day of the year was Jubilee Day, the twenty-first of June. . . . As we heard the waves of cheering roll over the city, we dreamed an impossible but not ignoble dream of world leadership, and rededicated ourselves to the service of a thrice–crowned queen.'

He Fell Among Thieves, a poem which Lord Curzon greatly admired, has as its subject a young Englishman condemned by his Asian captors to be killed but granted his wish to live till the dawn. He dies of course unflinchingly, but before he does so he has time to remember 'the April noon on his books aglow . . . the School Close, sunny and green, the runner beside him . . . the College Eight and their trainer aloof, the Dons on their dais serene'.

Newbolt's nationalism was not a narrow one. His acceptance of the imperial tradition precluded this, for by their very natures nationalism and imperialism must at times be incompatible. In 1907 a small group of men, of whom Newbolt was one, decided to form the English Association, a body whose aims were somewhat loosely defined but included the spread and cultivation of the English language. To Newbolt it seemed at first that the association could play a useful part in promoting that cultural, political and even, it might be said, moral unity of the English–speaking nations which as an ideal inspired Cecil Rhodes, John Buchan and others who had been lastingly influenced by the events of the South African war. (It was through Buchan's intercession that Newbolt was appointed by Lord Beaverbrook to the Ministry of Information in 1918. While working there Newbolt put forward one proposal which aroused Beaverbrook's enthusiasm. This was for the maintenance after the war of a wireless service of imperial news.)

One of the most attractive political figures to those who campaigned for either imperial or English–speaking unity was Field–Marshal Jan Christiaan Smuts, one–time rebel Boer commander and later firm ally of the British. At a dinner given by the British Ministry of Information in 1918 Smuts, consciously or unconsciously, echoed Newbolt's words and sentiments. In his speech he said: 'England made a mistake in 1776.' Newbolt interrupted him by calling out: 'And paid for it.'

'And paid for it', Smuts agreed and continued, 'and then made—I may perhaps be permitted to think—another mistake in 1899.'

'And paid again,' Newbolt called out.

Either through hardness of hearing or from an exquisite feeling of courtesy towards his interruptor Smuts added:

'And played the game.'

There were cheers all round.

One difficulty which confronted Newbolt and others who believed in the unity of the English–speaking peoples was the attitude commonly adopted towards it in Ireland, which to many of them seemed both mystifying and illogical. It may even have played a part in causing some of them to switch their allegiance from the English–speaking peoples to the so–called Anglo-Saxon races. In verse Newbolt offered what he evidently considered the only plausible explanation of Ireland and the Irish. This appears in the poem *Ireland, Ireland,* which contains the lines:

Still thy spirit wanders wailing,
Wanders wailing, wanders mad.

By 1928, the year in which he was elected President of the English Association, Newbolt had become somewhat apprehensive about current political trends in Britain, and like others who had shared his earlier enthusiasms he began to look outside the established political machinery for inspiration and some new form of organization. In his presidential address, after referring to the General Strike of 1926 as 'our nine days' civil war', he made an appeal for a national fellowship in which it would be possible for everyone to forget the existence of classes. He had, he said, given much thought during the preceding five years to the form which the new society should take, and he appealed to his audience for help in devising and putting into operation 'a scheme under which your Association would ally itself with all those men and women in every neighbourhood who have grasped the fact of today—the salient fact that the present form of society is wholly inadequate to find place for all who are able to create and worthy to enjoy an unembarrassed sense of nationality'.

Love for a country, an ideal, a school could all inspire Newbolt to poetry of a kind. Love for a woman could not. His wife Margaret seems, if we are to judge by J. H. M. Furse's bust, to have been a beautiful woman. She and Newbolt shared a full social life, and there is no reason for doubting that they enjoyed a satisfying and fulfilling marriage. To Newbolt these were subjects to be treated with reticence, and any expression of desire for any other woman was manifestly taboo. In reading his memoirs we find ourselves far advanced through his university days before we come to a mention of a girl. Then there is a brief reference to his dancing partner, a Miss Arnold, in an anecdote about John Ruskin, who entreated Newbolt and Miss Arnold to dance one more highland schottische. There follows a eulogy of the wisdom and skill as a hostess of Mrs Max Miller, who 'knew that attachments between young people of the undergraduate age were as likely as they were untimely, and . . . took great pains to keep the fun so open and so loud as to avert the perils of Commemoration Week'.

Newbolt's reticences and his references to women differ appreciably both in expression and spirit from those of puritans of earlier ages, many of whom took a positive delight in fulminating against women's wiles and weaknesses. His attitude was rather an expression of deference to a code, which had steadily been gaining acceptance in the upper middle class, and which ruled that outside certain clearly defined categories, such as mother, wife, sister and family friend, almost any form of communication with a woman was liable to be considered in questionable taste.

From Newbolt's writings and from Newbolt's life, which were exceptionally harmoniously blended, there emerges then a figure who is both an ideal and a reality. He is also the living embodiment of that message which, as much as a facility for rhyming, was the cause of the eminence which Newbolt's contemporaries accorded to him. Imbued with a strong sense of institutional loyalty, upper middle class by background, conformist in belief, dedicated to a concept, not simply of 'my country right or wrong', but of a nation enjoying a natural moral prerogative, accepting ungrudgingly the demands of service and duty, inclined to treat women either as companions or as unmentionable; add to this a natural power of command, some degree of worldly success, a distrust of latter-day politicians and a tendency towards philistinism in artistic taste, and we have the species *homo newboltiensis* or Newbolt Man. The ideal of the species was both happily and reverently described, appropriately enough, in a book entitled *Clifton School Days* by O. F. Christie:

> To be in all things decent, orderly, self-mastering; in action to follow up the coolest common sense with the most unflinching endurance; in public affairs to be devoted as a matter of course, self-sacrificing without any appearance of enthusiasm: on all social occasions—except at the regular Saturnalia—to play the Horatian man of the world, the Gentleman after the high Roman fashion, making a fine art, almost a religion, of Stoicism.

Cast in the role of hero, this figure dominated a large area of English literature, which may be loosely described as popular fiction, for about a century. How and why this was so, whence Newbolt Man, who does, of course, antedate Newbolt himself, came and why he disappeared will provide the subject of this book.

The frontiers of popular fiction are not altogether easily defined. Graham Greene offered a helpful guide when he classified certain of his novels as Entertainment, and this guide I intend in the main to follow. But in searching for the origins of Newbolt Man it will be necessary first to consider some works of a highly didactic nature, whose authors, writing primarily for the young, expressly stated that their intention was not so much to entertain as to moralize and to instruct.

CHAPTER ONE

Christian Socialism and Muscular Christianity

Tom Brown's School Days was first published in 1857. The name of the author, Thomas Hughes, did not appear on the title page, the book being attributed to 'an Old Boy'. By this device Hughes asserted his amateur status as a writer while proclaiming his allegiance to a peculiarly English concept, which differs from its Scottish counterpart, 'former pupil', both in being a contradiction in terms and in suggesting a desire for the perpetuation of adolescence.

The book is unashamedly didactic. In his preface Hughes wrote: 'I can't see that a man has any business to write at all unless he has something which he thoroughly believes and wants to preach about.' He also asked whether it was likely that someone who had reached his time of life—he was thirty-three when he began writing the book—who had his bread to earn and little time to spare would 'spend almost the whole of his yearly vacation in writing a story just to amuse people'.

One of the most celebrated passages in the book, and one in which the moral which Hughes was trying to preach emerges most clearly, is Squire Brown's soliloquy when he is considering what to say to his son just before putting him on the stage coach to Rugby.

'I won't tell him to read his Bible,' the squire says to himself, 'and love and serve God; if he don't do that for his mother's sake and teaching, he won't for mine. . . . If he'll only turn out a brave, helpful, truth–telling Englishman, and a gentleman, and a Christian, that's all I want.' In the end he says to Tom: 'You tell the truth, keep a brave and kind heart, and never listen to or say anything you wouldn't have your mother and sister hear, and you'll never feel ashamed to come home, or we to see you.'

Tom, moulded by the codes and practices of Rugby school, guided by the godlike headmaster who is referred to as 'the Doctor', and with the advantages of his own inherent nature, develops into just that character which his father wishes him to be. The character is Newbolt Man in boy or embryo form, clearly delineated, immediately popular, and later to be reproduced by countless other authors of books for boys.

Five editions of *Tom Brown's School Days* appeared in 1857, and seventy editions in Hughes's lifetime. Soon after it was published Charles Kingsley wrote to Hughes to tell him that the general opinion of readers was that 'it is the jolliest book they ever read'. That such an epithet as 'jolly' could be used was in itself a comment on many of the novels written for and about boys before 1857, or indeed for some time after.

One of the most popular forerunners of *Tom Brown's School Days* was Thomas Day's *The History of Sandford and Merton*, which was first published in 1789. In an introduction to this work Cecil Hartley stated that of all the writings for early youth that had come before the world since the appearance of *Robinson Crusoe* no other had afforded so much amusement, conveyed more valuable information or had so elevating an influence over the mind.

Day, like Hughes, was an idealist, his favourite cause being the improvement of the lot of negro slaves. He must also have been able to inspire strong personal affection, for following his early death after a riding accident, his widow took to her bed, never allowed the curtains of her room to be drawn again, and in about two years followed her husband to the grave. However, in Sandford and in Merton he created two small boys who must strike the modern reader as rather objectionable but who are nevertheless the joint heroes of the book.

Tommy Merton, who was born in Jamaica, has been spoilt by the attention of too many servants and on arriving in England at the age of six can neither read nor write, can use none of his limbs with ease, and is 'proud, fretful, and impatient'. Yet he is 'naturally a well-disposed, good-natured boy'. Harry Sandford, by contrast, is the son of a 'plain, honest farmer', and is 'active, strong, hardy and fresh-coloured'. He is also so contented with his lot that 'give him only a morsel of dry bread for his dinner, and he would be satisfied, though you placed sweetmeats, and fruit, and every other nicety, in his way'.

Harry saves Tommy from the embraces of a snake, and in gratitude Tommy's father arranges for the two boys to be educated together in the home of a local clergyman named Barlow. Education for Tommy consists partly in being called upon to emulate the superior examples of Harry and Mr Barlow, and partly in the drawing of morals from various tales of history and legend. Many of these emphasize the superiority of poor men who happily accept their station in life over rich men who are vain and greedy. There is something of a conflict when Tommy returns home, accompanied by Harry, and is surrounded by rich young friends who have attended public schools, where they have made the acquaintance of the young Lord Squander and have 'learned every vice and folly that are usually taught at such places'. For a time Tommy sides with the rich against his farm-boy friend, but once again danger threatens from the animal kingdom. The creature this time is a bull. Harry of course saves Tommy, and Harry in his turn is saved by a half-naked negro boy, who has recently appeared on the scene and to whom Harry earlier gave what was very nearly his last sixpence.

Sermonizer though Thomas Hughes was, *Tom Brown's School Days,* in realism, power of descriptive writing, delineation of character and readability is immeasurably superior to all this. The description of Tom Brown's journey to school by stage coach may owe something to Dickens, but there is nothing imitative in the account of the rugby football match which Tom witnesses soon after his arrival nor in many of the other school scenes. They are as authentic as the character of 'the head of the eleven, the head of big–side football', Peter Brooke, known as 'Old Brooke'. Old Brooke makes his speech at the house supper with 'no action, no tricks of oratory; plain, strong, and straight, like his play'.

'Then there's fuddling about in the public–house,' he says, 'and drinking bad spirits, and punch, and such rot–gut stuff. That won't make good drop–kicks or chargers of you, take my word for it. . . . Each of us knows and can depend on his next–hand man better —that's why we beat them today. We've union, they've division.'

The climax of the speech, greeted by frantic cheers, comes when Old Brooke declares that he would 'sooner win two School–house matches running than get the Balliol scholarship any day'.

East, Tom's first school friend, brandishing his knowledge of Rugby lore in order to impress the new boy Tom, is equally convincing, and though the bully Flashman is a stereotype, he too has survived, at least in name and in latter–day parodies. It is only in the portrayal of 'the Doctor' and of the egregious Arthur that Hughes's limitations as a novelist are fully exposed. These two serve mainly to provide Tom, the healthy, games–playing, middle-brow squire's son, with the reverse side of his spiritual coinage. The two sides together constitute Christianity as understood by a group of youngish men in the 1850s among whom Hughes was a leading figure.

To Hughes, and to Tom Brown, the Doctor, who is of course Thomas Arnold, is 'the true sort of captain . . . for a boys' army, one who had no misgivings, and gave no uncertain word of command, and, let who would yield or make truce, would fight the fight out (so every boy felt) to the last gasp and the last drop of blood'. The complexities of the real Thomas Arnold, that passionate, emotional, intellectual being, who could break down and weep in front of his whole school, and who was sufficiently radical in temperament to be able to state that his love for any place or person or institution was the exact measure of his desire to reform them, were beyond Hughes's powers to depict.

One of the most important services which the Doctor is considered to have rendered Tom was to make the clergyman's son, Arthur, Tom's study companion. Arthur startles the dormitory by kneeling down and saying his prayers, an action which prompts a bully to throw a slipper at him. Tom responds by throwing a boot at the bully, who, stamping with pain, roars:

> 'Confound you, Brown, what's that for?'
>
> 'Never mind what I mean', said Tom, stepping on to the floor, every drop of blood in his body tingling; 'if any fellow wants the other boot, he knows how to get it'.

That makes one dormitory safe for prayer, and before long Arthur has not only persuaded Tom to read the Bible diligently but has extracted a promise from him to give up using cribs. This last concession is granted after Arthur, on finally recovering from a prolonged fever, laid his 'thin white hand, on which the blue veins stood out so plainly, on Tom's great brown fist, and smiled at him'.

The Doctor and Arthur give Tom a few refinements, but he remains the same sturdy fighter, the kind of boy who would have one fight at school and after that need not have another. 'What,' Tom's creator comments in one of his didactic passages, 'would life be like without fighting? . . . Fighting, rightly understood, is the business, the real highest, honestest business of every son of man.' The enemies to be fought, he adds, include a man's evil thoughts and habits, wickedness in high places, Russians or border–ruffians, and those who will not let a man live his life in quiet until he has thrashed them.

In Tom, courage and readiness to fight for the right causes are accompanied by an unusually pronounced desire to retain as long as possible the status of schoolboy. Towards the end of the

book he even expresses the wish that the Doctor would allow him
to stay at school until the age of twenty. Could anyone picture Tom
Jones wanting to stay at a boys' boarding school until he was
twenty?

In 1858, the year after the publication of *Tom Brown's School
Days,* another book about a boys' school appeared which was also
to become a best-seller. This was *Eric or Little by Little,* by
Frederic William Farrar, the future headmaster of Marlborough
and archdeacon of Westminster. *Eric or Little by Little* is even more
explicitly a didactic work than *Tom Brown's School Days.* In a
preface to the twenty-fourth edition, which was published thirty-
one years after the first, Farrar wrote: 'The story of "Eric" was
written with but one single object—the vivid inculcation of moral
purity.' The story is that of the conflict between the forces of
good and evil as they take possession in turn of the soul of a
schoolboy named Eric Williams.

Soon after his arrival at Roslyn, a school based on King William's College at Castletown in the Isle of Man, where Farrar
himself was educated, Eric makes friends with a boy named Edwin
Russell. They and another boy are for a time the only ones in
their form to hold out against the practice of cribbing.

Eric begins to be led astray when he undergoes the experience
of being 'taken up' by an older boy. There is of course no suggestion that anything physical is associated with the process of
taking up. Nevertheloss the author deplores the practice. Eric is
taken up by 'a fine sturdy fellow of eighteen,' named Upton,
'who had a great notion of being manly, which he thought consisted in a fearless disregard of all rules'. Under Upton's influence
Eric describes a master as 'a surly devil', and Edwin is shocked to
hear a swear-word for the first time on Eric's lips.

Even worse influences are exerted by a boy named Ball, who
uses indecent words, and in the darkness of the dormitory Eric
finds himself 'blushing scarlet to the roots of his hair, and then
growing pale again, while a hot dew was left upon his forehead'.
Smoking is Eric's next serious lapse, and his kindly housemaster

is disturbed because he is getting into too many scrapes and letting boys beat him who are 'far your inferiors in ability'. But with the coming of the Easter holidays Eric has a chance to redeem himself.

He, Edwin Russell and another boy find themselves cut off by the tide. Eric has no difficulty in reaching safety, but Edwin is badly hurt and marooned on a rock. Displaying great courage, Eric drags Edwin to the shore, an action for which he is very properly awarded a medal by the Royal Humane Society, but Edwin's injuries are to prove fatal. In his delirium he is heard to say: 'Dear Eric, don't smoke.' Then 'the gentle, holy, pure spirit of Edwin Russell . . . passed into the presence of its Saviour and its God'.

Without Edwin Russell's earthly presence Eric finds temptation increasingly difficult to resist. A boy named Brigson appears on the scene who was expelled from 'one of the most ill-managed schools in Ireland', a fact which was 'treacherously concealed from the authorities'. Brigson is a bully and a coward, but he flatters Eric and in time persuades him to drink beer. From beer Eric and his new associates pass to brandy, and from brandy to an episode involving the theft of a couple of pigeons. One of the drinking set is the boy whom Eric has now taken up, a twelve-year-old named Wildney. Eric and Wildney are observed to be drunk at prayers, and the headmaster decides to expel both. He revokes this decision only after intercessions by those of Eric's friends who have been good influences, and on being reminded of the act which won Eric his medal for gallantry.

Once again Eric seems set on the right path. He and some of his old friends, with whom he is now in harmony, have an outing in a boat, taking with them 'nothing more objectionable' than ginger beer and lemonade, but once again death intervenes. The victim this time is Eric's younger brother Vernon, who is more than once described as 'a jolly little fellow', and whom Eric alternately befriended and neglected according to his moral outlook at the time. Vernon falls over a cliff while birds-nesting and is killed instantaneously. Eric writes to his aunt: 'Oh, how my whole soul yearns towards him. I *must* be a better boy, I *will* be better than I have been.'

Unfortunately such resolutions are not enough. 'Great as his trials had been,' we are told, 'it was God's will that he should pass through a yet fiercer flame ere he could be purified from pride and passion and self-confidence.' The landlord of the Jolly Herring, Eric's haunt in his drinking days, threatens him with exposure and demands payment for silence. Eric is tempted to steal from the funds controlled by the cricket treasurer. He narrowly resists the temptation, actually pocketing the money and then deciding to return it, but he finds that he has inadvertently failed to return a sovereign. When the money is shortly afterwards stolen by the Jolly Herring's landlord, who, being a former college servant, knows where to look, Eric is suspected by nearly everyone. Being unaware that all the money is missing, and not merely the one sovereign, which he has already thrown over a cliff, Eric decides he cannot face the prospect of expulsion once more and runs away to sea. As a cabin-boy aboard a trading schooner he is so brutally treated that when he finally makes his way home he is in a condition which causes him and everyone around him to know he is soon going to die. He lingers on long enough to learn that his mother, on hearing of Vernon's death and his own disgrace, has herself died from distress. Soon after this 'Eric was with those he dearliest loved, in the land where there is no more curse'.

Eric's failure to survive the effects of a fairly short stretch as a cabin-boy clearly puts him outside the category of Newbolt Man, even in Newbolt Man's most youthful form. Nor is he much of a fighter. When he is bullied in his early days at school it is his father, temporarily resident in the Isle of Man, and not Eric himself, who deals peremptorily with the bully.

Eric's positive attributes also differ from those of Newbolt Man. Whereas Tom Brown's mental equipment is just above public school average, Eric is fully aware that 'few of his fellows had gifts like his, either of mind or of person, and his fair face often showed a clear impression of his own superiority'. He is something of an aesthete, being 'fond of beauty in every shape,' and he and Vernon are both sufficiently sensitive to combine their praying frequently with weeping.

Yet for all the mawkishness of the tale and its narration, the gentleness of spirit, combined with the vigour of faith, which inspired *Eric or Little by Little* may well be considered a closer approximation to the message of the gospels than was the combative creed of Thomas Hughes. To those who are more familiar with the works of Dean Farrar the theologian than with the works of Farrar the novelist this may not seem surprising. But it was not with Eric Williams that boy readers in general in the late 1850s and through the next decade tended to identify themselves. Their choice was much more likely to be Tom Brown or another young hero, who was the creation of Hughes's close friend, the Reverend Charles Kingsley. This was Amyas Leigh, the hero of *Westward Ho!*

Westward Ho!, which was published two years before *Tom Brown's School Days,* is dedicated jointly to Sir James Brooke and George Augustus Selwyn. Brooke was the former servant of the East India Company, who, after inheriting a fortune, devoted himself to the task of rescuing the islands of the Indian archipelago from what he considered barbarism and became the Rajah of Sarawak. Selwyn was the hard–riding, swimming, sailing first Bishop of New Zealand, to whom a memorial was later erected in the form of a Cambridge college paid for by public subscription. The dedication, Kingsley wrote, was 'by one who (unknown to them) has no other method of expressing his admiration and reverence for their characters'. He went on:

> That type of English virtue, at once manful and godly, practical and enthusiastic, prudent and self–sacrificing, which he has tried to exhibit in these pages, they have exhibited in a form even purer and more heroic than that in which he has drest it, and than that in which it was exhibited by the worthies whom Elizabeth, without distinction of rank or age, gathered round her in the ever glorious wars of her great reign.

In *Westward Ho!* the enemies to be fought in straightforward battle are the Spaniards, and perhaps for that reason they are presented as superior beings to their English Roman Catholic sympathizers. Spanish sailors are guilty, it is true, of cruelty, in contrast with 'that tenderness towards the Indians, which is so striking a feature of the Elizabethan seamen', and which is largely attributable to 'their more liberal creed'. But the noble Spanish prisoner of war, Don Guzmán, behaves with dignity and has sufficient charm for the heroine, Rose Salterne, to fall, temporarily at least, in love with him. The martyr Edmund Campion, and Robert Parsons, by contrast, appear as 'Jesuits, and gentlemen in no sense in which that word is applied in this book'.

The clearest evidence of the effects of creed on character and conduct is to be found in Eustace Leigh, Amyas Leigh's Roman Catholic cousin. Eustace, like Amyas, desires Rose Salterne, but

> Eustace's love had little or nothing of chivalry, self-sacrifice, or purity in it; these were virtues which were not taught at Rheims. Careful as the Jesuits were over the practical morality of their pupils, their severe restraint had little effect in producing real habits of self-control. . . . He longed to marry Rose Salterne, with a wild, selfish fury; but only that he might be able to claim her as his own property. . . . Of her as a co-equal and ennobling helpmate; as one in whose honour, glory, growth of heart and soul, his own were inextricably wrapt up, he had never dreamed.

Apart from the blemish of a number of Roman Catholics, who form what later ages would know as a fifth column, the English have the privilege of living in 'noble days, when the chivalry of the middle age was married to the free thought and enterprise of the new'. The age precedes 'those worse times which began in the latter years of Elizabeth, and after breaking her mighty heart, had full licence to bear their crop of fools' heads in the profligate days of James'.

The men of Devon play an outstanding part in preventing England from becoming 'a Popish appanage of a world–tyranny as cruel as heathen Rome itself, and far more devilish'. Overcoming Spanish 'jealousy', they have, 'in true English fashion, won their markets at the sword's point, and then bought and sold honestly and peaceably therein'. Occasionally the English are obliged to take sterner measures than they might wish. Raleigh condemns seven hundred Spaniards to death, and the author comments: 'It was done. Right or wrong it was done. . . . The hint was severe, but it was sufficient.' There was also the mitigating circumstance that the incident. occurred in Ireland. (Kingsley found the Irish baffling. When he visited the country he affected to be surprised by discovering the inhabitants had white skins, and he even went so far as to describe them as 'white chimpanzees'.)

The principal English heroes in the book are joined together in a chivalrous union known as the Brotherhood of the Rose. They share a love for Rose Salterne and a desire to outstrip each other in loyalty to the Queen, valour against her foes, and deeds of courtesy and mercy to the afflicted and oppressed. One of the leading figures in the brotherhood is Amyas Leigh's elder brother Frank, a sophisticated courtier. Frank is well–read, artistic, loyal, brave, generous and cast in the Philip Sidney mould, but he is not the main hero of the book. This distinction belongs to Amyas.

Amyas Leigh is presented at once as a fighter in the right causes. Before he is fifteen he tells John Oxenham that though he has a boy's age he has a man's fist, and though he is a gentleman's son he would gladly serve as a cabin–boy on board Oxenham's ship in order to be able to fight the Spaniards. In his school days he 'hardly considered he had done his duty in his calling if he went home without beating a big lad for bullying a small one'.

Amyas comes of 'as good blood as any in Devon', and it is of the country rather than the town variety. He speaks 'like Raleigh, Grenvile, and other low persons, with a broad Devonshire accent'. A little Latin has been drummed into him by repeated blows, but the only books he knows are the Bible, the Prayer Book, the old *Mort d'Arthur* and Las Casas's history of the West Indies 'lately

done into English under the title of "The Cruelty of the Spaniards'". His religion too is plain and uncomplicated. He says his
creed and the Lord's prayer night and morning, attends church daily,
and reads the day's psalms with his mother every evening. He has
learnt from both his parents that it is 'infinitely noble to do right
and infinitely base to do wrong', but he knows 'nothing more of
theology, or of his own soul, than is contained in the Church
Catechism'.

Great physical strength and courage are combined in Amyas
with the ability to inspire loyalty. The old campaigner Salvation
Yeo attaches himself to Amyas as a devoted and uncomplaining
bodyguard, and during their voyage to the West Indies the elder
brother Frank admires the way in which Amyas, 'without genius,
scholarship, or fancy, had gained, by plain honesty, patience, and
common sense, a power over the human heart'. Amyas also has
those real habits of self–control which the Jesuits failed to instil
into their pupils. He returns after three years' overseas service 'as
pure as the day he was born, having been trained, as many a brave
young man was then, to look upon profligacy, not as a proof of
manhood, but as . . . a cowardly and effeminate sin'.

In a letter to J. M. Ludlow, Kingsley wrote of a friend from
his undergraduate days, Frank Penrose: 'He is my model for my
hero in *Westward Ho!*, and I want none better, for I believe him
to be incapable of meanness or vanity.' After admitting that Penrose
was unimaginative, he added: 'His eye is single, and his heart is
mighty in warmth, though not in heat.' Of Amyas Leigh Kingsley
wrote:

> As he stands there with beating heart and kindling eye, the
> cool breeze whistling through his long fair curls, he is a symbol,
> though he knows it not, of brave young England longing to
> wing its way out of its island prison, to discover and to traffic,
> to colonise and to civilise until no wind can sweep the earth
> which does not bear the echoes of an English voice.

Sir Henry Newbolt could not have wished for a better model.

Hughes and Kingsley may or may not have been the earliest begetters of young Newbolt Man, for whether earlier examples are to be found in English fiction must be a matter of subjective judgment. But that two such clearly delineated young heroes as Tom Brown and Amyas Leigh should have been created nearly concurrently by two writers who were not only close friends, but who shared so many religious, political and social beliefs, is surely significant. It suggests at least that a consideration of those beliefs, and of how the two men translated them into practice, may give some clue as to why Newbolt Man appeared in fiction when he did and in the form he did.

Hughes, like his hero Tom Brown, was educated at Rugby. Like Tom Brown too he captained the Rugby school cricket eleven and in a match against an M.C.C. team led by Lord Charles Russell, after going in first, 'to give his men pluck', showed his versality in the field by bowling one man and stumping another. From Rugby he went on to Oxford, where in collaboration with his brother George, who stroked an Oxford crew to victory against Cambridge, he wrote a song, of which the last two lines were:

Row and work, boys of England, on rivers and seas,
And the old land shall hold, firm as ever, her own.

Soon after coming down from Oxford Thomas Hughes was attracted to Christian Socialism, a movement with high ideals created largely by middle–class professional men, of whom the guiding spirit from the outset was Frederick Dennison Maurice, professor of English literature and history, and later too of divinity, at King's College in the University of London, and a man of exceptional intellectual gifts. In explaining what he himself could bring to the movement Hughes stated: 'I am not much of a thinker or projector. . . . I think it is more fit that I should take my full whack as executor and, if necessary, . . . endurer.'

This he duly did. At the Working Men's College in Red Lion Square, which was Maurice's creation, Hughes insisted that all the pupils should box him in turn, and cricket and rowing clubs were soon established. Hughes's reputation as an athlete was readily recognized by the leaders of Christian Socialism as an appreciable asset.

The aspects of Christian Socialism which attracted Hughes most strongly were cooperative societies and trade unionism. He was an active supporter of the Amalgamated Society of Engineers during the prolonged lock–out of 1852, a form of partisanship which required both courage and independence of judgment in a man of his social position. One of his many attractive qualities was his readiness to spend his own money, although he was never a rich man, on the causes in which he believed, and his support of the cooperative efforts of working tailors cost him about £1,000. The republicanism which a number of socialists of the time favoured was, on the other hand, something he was not willing to tolerate, and at a meeting held in 1849 there was a critical moment when a number of Chartists hissed the national anthem. Hughes leapt on to a chair and announced that the first man who hissed the Queen's name would have to settle accounts with him personally. Nobody did, the piano struck up, and the loyal singing was resumed.

It was characteristic of Hughes that in 1859 he raised two companies of volunteers from the Working Men's College, and when the Queen reviewed these troops the next year he was already formally in command. His feelings of patriotism, like those of others who sympathized with his opinions, were noticeably strengthened by the outbreak of the Crimean war, and he became more and more concerned with the advocacy of a strong Anglo-American alliance which, together with the Cape Colony and Australia, would, as he expressed it, produce 'a chain of free English–speaking nations which would have little trouble making their will respected and keeping the world's peace for the rest of time, or till Armageddon at any rate'.

The cause of Anglo–American friendship was one to which Hughes devoted himself in a number of enterprises which were characteristic of his impulsive and generous nature. The least harmful of these was a boat race on the Thames between an Oxford and a Harvard crew, which he umpired. The saddest, in the outcome, was his establishment of a new community in eastern Tennessee. This was a cooperative venture, whose controlling body was a board of aid to land ownership, of which Hughes was president. The township to be formed was given the name of Rugby. The start was encouraging. A ceremonial inauguration took place in the presence of the Mayor of Chattanooga and the Bishop of Tennessee, the congregation singing Jerusalem the Golden. Unfortunately Rugby, Tennessee, soon came to be used largely as a dumping ground for young Englishmen whose families considered that, if they were ever to benefit from anything, it might be from the strict regulations imposed in the community on the sale of alcohol. When the supplies of Worcester sauce ran out and it was realized that the nature of the Tennessee soil was such that it might never be possible to produce good lawn tennis courts, the community entered into a decline from which it never recovered.

Imprudent though he sometimes was, Hughes's career, like that of a number of other writers who were also begetters of Newbolt Man, was one of appreciable worldly success. As his biographers, Mack and Armytage, pointed out, he had by the age of forty–eight been a member of Parliament, president of the first Cooperative Congress, chairman of the Crystal Palace Company, a Q.C. and the author of a best–selling novel. This was an appreciable haul for a man who had described himself as not much of a thinker or projector. His success continued, and after he left politics he was made a county court judge. But his fame today derives almost entirely from his first book, the most famous novel on the subject of a boys' school in the English, and perhaps in any language. One man who readily acknowledged its influence on his thinking, and who came to Rugby school as if on a visit to a shrine, was Baron Pierre de Coubertin, the founder of the modern Olympic Games. It is questionable whether the Games would have been revived in their present form, particularly with the insistence on amateurism, if the baron had not encountered Hughes's work.

In 1876 Hughes gave a series of lectures at the Working Men's

College, which were published three years later under the title *The Manliness of Christ*. It was a title which might have been chosen specifically to appeal to Hughes's friend the Reverend Charles Kingsley.

Kingsley rated Hughes's judgment and common sense highly. He once wrote to tell him that he was 'the only man of our lot except Maurice, who seems to have the wildest sense of which way the cat jumps'. This he attributed to Hughes's pursuit of three of the four royal F's, namely fishing, fowling and foxhunting. But though the two agreed on the fundamental issue of what constituted a good Christian, they differed in their attitudes to such matters as ritual and outward appearances. Hughes dismissed arguments about ecclesiastical vestments as 'all this millinery business'. To Kingsley any division within the Church of England was likely to be a cause for concern and, not infrequently, for combat.

It is difficult today to feel much sympathy with Kingsley in his public debates with John Henry Newman or with other eminent men who, as he did, professed and called themselves Christians, albeit with different allegiances and perhaps from different motives. Contentious polemics on the question of which is the true interpreter of a faith shared by both parties are seldom productive of charitable thinking or edifying reading. But it has to be admitted that in Kingsley a particular brand of Anglican Christianity, in which he believed intensely and which appealed with no less force to others who were not so articulate as he was, had a champion with rich literary gifts which he used to exercise considerable powers of persuasion.

To many of his contemporaries, Kingsley, especially in his younger days, seemed a dangerous radical. In his early novel *Yeast* he presented a picture of rural life which cried out for reform, and in *Alton Locke* the urban misery depicted was equally convincing. (He did, it is true, become much less radical after he had achieved a considerable measure of worldly success, including appointments as chaplain-in-ordinary to the queen and, somewhat improbably, regius professor of modern history at Cambridge. But it would be too facile to attribute the change in outlook wholly to changes in circumstances. Kingsley genuinely believed the social order was altered for the better in the second half of the century.) There were also those who felt Kingsley took too lenient a view of youthful indulgence, and Tennyson was disturbed by his use of the word 'naked' and having to read that in the historical novel Hypatia was 'stript'.

Kingsley had no truck with strict sabbatarianism, and as a parent he differed sufficiently from posterity's stereotype of the Victorian father to be able to write: 'It is difficult enough to keep the Ten Commandments, without raising an eleventh in every direction.'

These were different facets of a rich and in many respects generous nature, but to none of his other causes did he devote himself with the same passionate intensity as he did to that of preserving the Church of England from what he believed to be dangerous and pernicious doctrines. There were at the time influential reformers within the Church with new ascetic and aesthetic values, proclaiming belief in monasticism, celibacy, confession, the power of absolution and a variety of ritual and doctrinal changes. It was in these men that Kingsley found the Church's principal enemies within. Beyond was an even more powerful enemy with which battle had to be joined, the Church of Rome, and Kingsley's reading of history was such that he found Roman Catholicism barely compatible with the patriotism of an Englishman.

To Kingsley, as to Hughes, patriotism became a subject of increasing concern in the second half of the century. Of the Crimean war, he wrote: 'Beside this war, one has no heart to sing of anything . . . and of it I cannot sing.' The Indian Mutiny also stirred strong emotions in Kingsley, leading him into a serious disagreement with his friend Ludlow, one of the most effective of the early Christian Socialists, over what Kingsley called 'colonial questions, as between the English man and the savage or foreigner'. The unity of the English–speaking races was for Kingsley, as for Hughes, an extension of patriotism, yet ¶t was the cause of yet another quarrel, this time between Kingsley and Hughes himself. Hughes was deeply committed to the Federal cause in the American Civil War, whereas Kingsley, largely because of his contemptuous attitude towards negroes, favoured the South.

When attacking his ecclesiastical enemies Kingsley frequently coupled their apparent lack of patriotism with the charge of effeminacy, a word he used with remarkable frequency. In his introduction to his early poetic work, *The Saint's Tragedy,* he expressed the hope that it might divert at least one young reader from 'the example of those miserable dilettanti, who in books and sermons are whimpering meagre second-hand praises of celibacy'. In a letter to a young clergyman he described the 'so-called' saintliness of Roman Catholic priests as 'a poor pitiful thing . . . not God's ideal of a man, but an effeminate shaveling's ideal'. Of Newman and his followers he wrote: 'In him, and in all that school, there is an element of foppery—even in dress and manner; a fastidious, maundering, die-away effeminacy.' He even described the age in which he lived as an effeminate one, which would 'pardon the lewdness of the gentle and sensitive vegetarian, while it has no mercy for that of the sturdy peer, proud of his bull-neck and his boxing'—a somewhat unorthodox picture of mid-Victorian society.

What exactly did Kingsley mean by effeminacy? His biographer, R.B. Martin, like others before him, has suggested that the strength of Kingsley's feeling on the subject probably derived in part from alarming suspicions of homosexual tendencies in his brother Henry. This may well have been so. Charles Kingsley certainly had an unashamed delight in the physical pleasures of marriage, as his letters to his wife indicate, and phrases such as 'prayer-mongering eunuchs', which he used readily, seem to have significance, if only because he must have known that the men to whom he was referring were not in fact eunuchs. Which of those ordained priests in the Church of England or the Roman Catholic Church whom Kingsley regarded as enemies had homosexual tendencies, which, if any, indulged in homosexual practices, and how much Kingsley knew or suspected, must be subject to doubt, largely because of the limitations of the permissible phraseology of the time. We can only be certain that Kingsley was attacking the antithesis of what Hughes called the manliness of Christ, and he was never more combative than when doing so.

The term used to describe this doctrine of the manliness of Christ which passed into common currency was muscular Christianity. (An anonymous contributor to the *Saturday Review* seems to have been the first to use it.) Kingsley claimed that he did not know what muscular Christianity meant, describing it in a sermon as 'a clever expression, spoken in jest by I know not whom'. To many of Kingsley's contemporaries, however, and to posterity, the concept of muscular Christianity was clear enough. For a physical embodiment of it they had no need to look further than Kingsley himself or Thomas Hughes, and for fictional embodiments to their two young heroes, Tom Brown and Amyas Leigh.

The links between muscular Christianity and Newbolt Man, particularly in his earliest manifestations, are evident. So too are the links between muscular Christianity and Christian Socialism. That Newbolt Man should have had his origins in socialism of any kind, Christian or secular, is a thesis which would have puzzled both Newbolt and Newbolt's Fabian contemporaries. Yet it is almost certainly true.

CHAPTER TWO

Penny Dreadfuls and the Ballantyne Boy

Tom Brown's School Days and *Eric or Little by Little* were both best-sellers, and each provided a formula for success by writers who followed in the wake of Hughes and of Farrar. But for all the popularity of the new fashions in schoolboy novels young readers of English fiction in the late 1850s and the 1860s were certainly not restricted to a choice between the pallid pieties of Eric Williams and his like and the muscular pieties of Tom Brown and his like. In fact the young readers of the period in very large numbers opted rather for the so-called penny dreadful, a literary genre which flourished particularly strongly in the 1840s.

Penny dreadfuls had their origin in part in the highly popular accounts of crime and criminals assembled in the *Newgate Calendar*. At their most successful they served to perpetuate a central character, not infrequently a criminal, through millions of words and several decades. A popular penny dreadful of the 1840s, for example, was *Varney the Vampire* or *The Feast of Blood,* which preceded Bram Stoker's *Dracula* by about half a century. In *Varney the Vampire* Victorian children could read:

> The glassy horrible eyes of the figure ran over the angelic form with a hideous satisfaction—horrible profanation. He drags

her head to the bed's edge. He forces it back by the long hair still entwined in his grasp. With a plunge he seizes her neck in his fanglike teeth—a gush of blood and a hideous sucking noise follows.

This detailed description of an unusual variety of oral satisfaction does not seem to have invited any form of prosecution. Indeed its author, James Malcolm Rymer, in a preface to a new edition of the work published in 1847, was able to record: 'To the whole of the Metropolitan Press for their laudatory notices the author is particularly obliged.' Rymer, it is believed, was at one time sustaining ten serial stories simultaneously.

There was also Thomas Prest's Sweeney Todd, whose adventures were first recorded in a work entitled *The String of Pearls (A Romance)*. Todd is, of course, the notorious barber of Fleet Street, who murders his customers and despatches their bodies to a basement, where they are turned into pies by a young man imprisoned there. These are later sold by the female owner of a pie-shop.

The law eventually catches up with Sweeney Todd, but he has a long run before this happens, and readers are not spared much:

> The throng of persons in the shop looked petrified, and after Mrs Lovett's shriek there was an awful silence for about a minute, and then the young man who officiated as cook spoke.
>
> Ladies and gentlemen, I fear what I am going to say will spoil your appetites; but truth is beautiful at all times, and I have to state that Mrs Lovett's pies are made of *human flesh!*

The most successful dreadfuls were those which recorded the exploits of highwaymen and housebreakers and which were based, more or less accurately, on real-life incidents and characters. Their price made them accessible to large numbers of young readers, and competition was stimulated when some publishers were able to bring out dreadfuls at a halfpenny.

E.S. Turner, who in *Boys Will Be Boys,* produced an illuminating study of the subject, wrote of the readers of penny dreadfuls:

Wage slaves had no intention of spending their scanty leisure reading about wage slaves. Their spirit craved a more powerful stimulus. They wanted to read about fiery individualists, men of spirit who defied harsh laws and oppressive officialdom, even though they finished at the end of a hempen rope.

He was probably right, though the readership of penny dreadfuls was certainly not confined to wage slaves and probably included an appreciable proportion of the male upper and middle classes at some stage in their intellectual development.

The victims of Dick Turpin, the highwayman hero of numerous penny dreadfuls, are liable to be given such unattractive names as Ezekiel Funge, Lord Mayor of London, and Turpin transgresses other codes beside that of the sanctity of property. In one immensely popular serial story, *The Blue Dwarf,* he is described as 'partial to female company', the author even adding: 'For a family man Dick was particularly lax in his observances. But then he was away from home, and playing the bachelor.'

Charles Peace, the burglar who shot a policeman; Jack Sheppard, another notorious housebreaker; and a highwayman with supernatural powers known as Spring–Heeled Jack were also popular characters. Then towards the end of the 1850s, more or less contemporaneously with Eric Williams and Tom Brown, a new figure emerged in the world of penny dreadfuls, named Charley Wag. His originality derived from the fact that he was a boy, not an adult, burglar.

A more uplifting moral tone was discernible, it is true, a decade or so after the appearance of Tom Brown in serialized works for boys. An example is to be found in the adventures of the famous schoolboy hero, Jack Harkaway, who first emerged in the magazine *Boys of England* in 1871, and whose creator, Bracebridge Hemyng, was a respectable barrister. Yet even Jack Harkaway, when first encountered, is still far removed from Newbolt Man in embryo form. He tries to avoid corporal punishment, he is a forger and ventriloquist who can imitate masters' voices, he ignores the Queensberry rules when fighting other boys, he gambles heavily and loses, and he is 'spoony' on a girl called Little Emily, whom he actually kisses.

Of Jack's attitude to school his author writes: 'His wish was to get away, at all hazards, from the tyranny under which he groaned.' When his housemaster's wife asks him, 'how would you like to have me for a Mama?' he makes it clear he is having none of that and replies: 'I would rather have you for—for—'

A few decades later Jack Harkaway has become a different being. In the South African war he serves as a captain of hussars, and in one of his reincarnations as a schoolboy he says to a foreign-looking boy with thoroughly orthodox cruelty: '"You're not a true Englishman. . . . There's a touch of the tarbrush about you which shows you are not a white man."' But by then not only Jack Harkaway had changed; so too had the moral climate within which works of entertainment for boys were written.

An important influence in bringing about the change was the work of R.M. Ballantyne, whose popularity as a writer of adventure stories for boys also dates from the late 1850s. In his biography, *Ballantyne the Brave,* Eric Quayle wrote of Ballantyne's novels that 'for the first time in the annals of English juvenile literature, youngsters were able to identify themselves with the heroes of the tale they were reading'. It was they, he went on, who rescued helpless natives from cannibals or plunged into shark–infested waters to save an injured friend; they who modestly refused 'to accept any thanks from the erstwhile victim other than perhaps a firm shake from the gratefully outstretched hand'.

Any critic who unequivocally claims for any writer the distinction of having been first in a particular field is making a risky preemptive bid. There were certainly authors writing for the young when Ballantyne himself was still a child, who placed their boy heroes in dangerous and exciting situations. One such was Captain

Frederick Marryat, whose highly popular *Mr Midshipman Easy*, for example, was published in 1836, when Ballantyne was only eleven. Yet Marryat, despite all the skill with which, in narrative and descriptive passages, he drew on the experiences of his own adventurous life, was still too fettered by the demands of the didactic to be able to sustain for long that identification of boy reader with boy hero which Ballantyne undoubtedly achieved.

Marryat's *Masterman Ready,* which was first published in 1841, is the story of the Seagrave family, who are shipwrecked while on passage to Australia and find refuge on a desert island together with Masterman Ready, an elderly and God-fearing seaman. Mr Seagrave is described as 'a very well–informed clever man', and his eldest son William is the boy hero of the book, the other children serving mainly to provide a rather heavy form of comic relief.

The castaways have plenty of adventures in making the island habitable by man, and towards the end they are attacked by savage natives. William finds himself at the centre of the battle and comports himself as would be expected, but throughout the book he is never more than a secondary hero. The central figure is the old seaman Ready, an Admirable Crichton who knows his place.

'What's the first thing we must do, Ready?' inquired Mr Seagrave.

'Tomorrow we had better fix up another tent or two.'

. . . 'And what shall I do, Ready?' said Mr Seagrave.

'Why, sir, if you will have the kindness to sharpen the axe and the hatchet on the grindstone, it would be of great service.'

Even on a desert island William has to suffer the kind of instruction which was meted out in substantial chunks to Sandford and Merton. Ready teaches him ornithology, and his father explains to him the basic principles of zoology.

'The Almighty has filled the earth with living things; so long as they do not interfere with man, they enjoy their portion of it in peace and quiet. As soon as man requires the territory, as they were made for his use and to be subservient to him, they must retrograde away from him, or be destroyed by him. Such is the will of a great and beneficent Creator.'

There is even some speculation about the political future when William asks: "'Will England ever fall, and be of no more importance than Portugal is now?'" Mr Seagrave, carefully weighing the evidence, as is his habit, replies: "'History tells us that such is the fate of all nations. We must, therefore, expect that it will one day be the fate of our dear country. At present we see no appearance of it . . . but, sooner or later, England will no more be mistress of the seas, or boast of her possessions all over the world.'"

In *Masterman Ready* there is a secondary plot, Ready's own life story which he relates at intervals throughout the book. Like Marryat himself, Ready ran away to sea when he was a boy, and he later describes how he and two other English boys became captives of the Dutch near the Cape of Good Hope. A Dutch farmer treats them cruelly, and the boys seize two muskets and a knife and prepare to escape. The farmer strikes one of the boys, Hastings, with a rhinoceros whip. Ready's other companion tells the Dutchman that if he strikes one more blow they will shoot him, and the young Ready then joins in.

"'Yes," cried I, "we are only boys, but you've Englishmen to deal with.'"

As soon as Hastings is freed he seizes a large wooden mallet, used for driving in stakes, and strikes the Dutchman down, crying out as he does so: "'That for flogging an Englishman, you rascal!'"

This is clearly an instance of boys being directly involved in adventure overseas, even though it is conveyed through the reminiscences of an old man, but here too the narrative has to be interrupted for a piece of moralizing. When Ready relates how he and his two companions stole some arms from Hottentots, William asks: "'Did you not do wrong to steal the Hottentot's musket?'"

Ready explains that he was in enemy territory and appeals to Mr Seagrave for arbitration. Mr Seagrave, after due deliberation, affirms that '"when two nations are at war, the property of either, when taken, is confiscated"'.

In *Masterman Ready* there are a number of expressions of pride in nationality. The English boys in Ready's narrative are different from other boys because they are English. But in comparison with novels of overseas adventure written for boys in later decades, in which Mr Seagrave's judicious speculations about England's future prospects would have been hardly conceivable, the pride seems remarkable before all else for its balance and restraint.

One of the most enchanting examples of the nineteenth-century short story, a genre in which the English produced relatively little of excellence, is Marryat's *S.W. and by W. ¾ W.* It is the story of a love affair between a young naval officer and a wind. The affair begins when the young man is ordered by his commander-in-chief and uncle to box the compass. This he has never been able to do, but by a lucky chance he learns what the direction of the wind is and comes up with the right answer, which is S.W. and by W. ¾ W. He thereupon vows never to mention any other wind by name again. He is later killed in action, and during the funeral service the wind shifts into his favourite quarter. 'The rain which descended were the tears which she shed at the dead of the handsome but not over-gifted lover.'

The name of the young naval officer is Jack Littlebrain, 'as handsome a boy as ever was seen, but it must be acknowledged that he was not very clever'. Before becoming a midshipman his chief employment was 'kissing and romping with the maids at home'. He becomes known as the greatest fool in his ship, yet 'the ladies observed, that such might possibly be the case, but at all events he was the handsomest young man in the Mediterranean fleet'.

Jack Littlebrain does not belong to the species *homo new-boltiensis*. Nor does Masterman Ready, nor even the young William. Perhaps Captain Marryat had observed the seamen of his time too closely and was too faithful a recorder of what he saw to create the prototype. Ballantyne by contrast found in the ideals of New-bolt Man a continual source of inspiration, and the typical Ballantyne boy was to become one of the most widely admired upholders of these ideals in the realms of juvenile fiction.

In Ballantyne's novel *The Lifeboat* there are three heroes. One is Guy Foster, whom we first encounter when he is aged twenty and described as 'tall, handsome and hearty'. This is in contrast to his uncle, Mr Denham the shipowner, who is 'starched, proud and portly'. The second hero is a youngish skipper in Denham's service, John Bax, a 'modest, lion–hearted British sailor', whose character is 'grave, straightforward and simple'. The third is a boy named Tommy Bogey, who has been brought up among the boatmen of Deal and who hero–worships Bax. Under Bax's influence Tommy begins to 'display, in unusual vigour, those daring, enthusiastic qualities which, although mingled with much that is evil, are marked characteristics of our seamen'. He also has some useful physical attributes, such as being 'singularly fleet of foot'.

Guy, Bax and Tommy all have a wide experience of shipwreck and other dangers, and each in turn achieves the unusual distinction of being awarded the Royal National Life–boat Institution's gold medal for gallantry. Their first adventure together occurs when Bax, courageously assisted by Tommy, saves the life of a girl named Lucy Burton, the daughter of a missionary. Then the schooner which Bax commands goes aground on the Goodwin Sands, the rescue this time being effected by the crew of the Broadstairs lifeboat. Guy informs his parsimonious uncle that the reason for the loss of the schooner was her unseaworthy condition and lack of suitable equipment. The uncle thereupon dismisses him from the firm.

Guy's mother has a neat little cottage in Deal, where a 'bright–faced, fair–haired girl' named Amy Russel has been brought up. She too has had first–hand experience of shipwreck. This occurred off the coast of Kent, when she and a number of other passengers were taken off by lifeboat. The lifeboat, on approaching the shore, capsized, but a 'tall stripling . . . shot like a rocket head–foremost into the sea'. The tall stripling was Guy Foster.

The presence of Amy Russel and of Lucy, the missionary's daughter, allows a lightly outlined love interest to be introduced. Guy loves Lucy, Lucy loves Guy, Bax loves Amy, and Amy loves Bax. Unfortunately Bax is under the impression that it is not he whom Amy loves but Guy, and the misunderstanding remains unresolved because Bax cannot bring himself to mention Amy's name to his friend. Bax therefore decides to seek his fortune in Australia. Tommy, still the ardent hero–worshipper, follows him and has a variety of adventures on the way out. He is the sole survivor of a collier wrecked because her skipper was addicted to rum, sails the vessel single–handed for a time, and is eventually picked up by a ship bound for Australia.

Bax and a friend have meanwhile toiled steadily. They have read the Bible to each other in the evenings, and they have managed to find a little gold. Soon after Tommy joins them they all three decide to return to England. One more shipping disaster has to be overcome, with Guy this time taking the place of an injured member of the crew of the Deal lifeboat. Finally Denham dies intestate, and Guy through his mother succeeds to the business. He makes sure all his ships are seaworthy and properly equipped and contributes handsomely to the Royal National Life–boat Institution.

The Lifeboat is as didactic a work as *Tom Brown's School Days*. The author's main purpose was to extol the merits of the lifeboat service, but he has other axes to grind. He repeatedly warns against the evils of strong drink, and at one point he breaks off the narrative to call attention to the importance of carrying 'our flag, our merchandise, and our Bibles to the ends of the earth'.

Martin Rattler, another young Ballantyne hero, who appears in the novel of the same name, proves his fighting qualities by taking on the school bully, who is proposing slowly to drown a white kitten belonging to the aunt who brought Martin up. The fight is witnessed by an Irish sailor, Barney O'Flannagan, with whom Martin strikes up a friendship and whose stories excite his imagination.

When he is fourteen years old Martin is swept out to sea in a small punt, but he is rescued by a seaman who jumps overboard from a ship on passage to Brazil. The seaman turns out to be Barney O'Flannagan, and Martin accompanies him to Brazil. Among his adventures in Brazil is an attack by a vampire bat. He is nursed back to health in a hermit's cave, but the hermit and his fellow-countrymen still have much to learn.

'"Yes," the hermit says, "Brazil, my country, wants the Bible."'

Martin is enslaved for several months by an Indian tribe, but he escapes by plunging over a steep precipice into a pool. In the end he, like Guy Foster, becomes a rich man, and when he has done so he spends his leisure in visiting the poor and reading the Bible to the sick.

In his views on the upbringing of boys Ballantyne was very much in line with Thomas Hughes. 'I firmly believe,' he wrote, 'that boys were intended to encounter all kinds of risks in order to prepare them to meet and grapple with the risks and dangers incident to a man's career with cool, cautious self-possession.' By contrast the boy who is 'muff' will, when he becomes a man, 'find himself unable to act in the common emergencies of life; to protect a lady from insolence; to guard his house from robbery; or to save his own child should it chance to fall into the water'.

Ballantyne's chosen way of life fully entitled him to express opinions on the effects of early hardship on the formation of character. As a young apprentice in the service of the Hudson's Bay Company in Canada he tracked for sixty-six days across rivers, lakes and uninhabited forest, averaging more than thirty-five miles a day. At the age of twenty-one he was in sole charge of one of the company's trading posts. Nor did later literary success deter him from facing discomfort. In order to ensure that his treatment of the subject was authentic he stayed aboard a lightvessel for seven days, during which he was continually seasick, and later he had a fortnight of seasickness aboard a trawler when preparing to write a book about the work of the Mission to Deep Sea Fishermen.

He became an author almost by accident when a friend of his mother's offered to pay for the publication of the letters he had sent home from Canada. After the failure of his second book he did not attempt to write for publication again for some years, and Eric Quayle was of the opinion that 'Ballantyne secretly longed to be recognized, not as a prosaic writer of juvenile fiction, but as the sort of figure revealed in the frontispiece—a ruggedly good-looking he-man, fearless and bold and the scourge of the ungodly'.

The muscularity of Kingsley's Christianity is firmly reproduced in Ballantyne's writings and beliefs, but in place of Kingsley's broad church Anglicanism and relative indulgence in good living there is a sterner Scottish presbyterianism and a dedication to that form of abstention which was so oddly called temperance. At the age of twenty-four Ballantyne was elected an elder of the Free Church of Scotland. At sixty-one he resigned from the Harrow Liberal Club when the committee passed a resolution permitting the sale of alcoholic drinks on club premises.

Throughout his life Ballantyne was exceptionally shy in the presence of girls, especially pretty ones. Like Gladstone he was addicted to the practice of accosting prostitutes and talking to them of Jesus, and in his writings even his worst villains behave towards women in the manner in which he, and presumably the bulk of his readers, would have considered gentlemanly.

Shyness in the presence of girls, satisfaction derived from a life of pioneering and adventure, a somewhat stern moral outlook, a desire for amateur rather than professional status as a practitioner of the arts, belief in the efficacy of rigorous training for boys, and acceptance—though not uncritical acceptance—of a social order in which prosperity was likely to be the reward of virtue—all these qualities were compatible with, and some were essential ingredients of, the character of Newbolt Man. There was too another characteristic of the typical Ballantyne boy, which recurs again and again

in the annals of Newbolt Man and which to modern sensibilities
is much less attractive. This is the ability to derive continual pleasure
from the slaughter of wild animals. In *The Gorilla Hunters* Ballantyne's three boy heroes, Ralph Rover, Jack Martin and Peterkin
Gray, are particularly badly afflicted with this lust for destruction.

'"Come," cried Jack at length, having lost patience and springing
forward, "if he won't attack us we must attack him."'

One of the boys estimates that they have bagged thirty–three
gorillas.

'"Thirty–six, if you count the babies in arms," responded
Peterkin.

' . . . . "Pity we didn't make up the forty," observed Jack.'

Martin Rattler did, it is true, go to considerable lengths to save
a white kitten, but that was a domestic pet. The gorillas were not.

The very popularity of Ballantyne's books helped to make them
an effective counterweight to the penny dreadful, but to many
people concerned with the welfare of the young in the 1860s this
counterweight did not seem enough.

Penny dreadfuls were also known as 'bloods', a name which
for some reason was thought to confer a greater dignity on them.
In the twentieth century a belief grew up that, in contrast with
more dangerous influences to which the young had since become
subject, the reading of bloods never did anyone any real harm. In
his preface to E.S. Turner's *Boys Will Be Boys,* which was published in 1948, Captain C.B. Fry, classical scholar and director of
the training ship *Mercury,* who in his time played cricket for
England, set the long–jump record for the world and was reputed
to have been short–listed for the Albanian throne, wrote:

> Silly cinema, cretinous croon–words have a deleterious
> effect. The cinema of the baser sort and the moronic verbosity
> of the crooner, are ten times worse than any Blood could be.

Such equanimity on the subject of bloods was not so readily
felt seventy or eighty years earlier.

In all ages in which young people have been exposed to new

forms of art or entertainment designed to appeal to the masses there has been widespread alarm at the likely effect on their morals. In England in the third quarter of the nineteenth century, when battle was waged strenuously for the souls of adult men, concern for the souls of boys was understandably acute.

The impressive growth in the number of public schools during the first half of Queen Victoria's reign was in itself evidence of this. These schools have often, and convincingly, been explained as a response to various social and economic pressures, including the accepted need to turn manufacturers' sons into gentlemen as expeditiously as possible. With hindsight the schools have also been seen as a forcing ground for a new breed of administrators, numbers of whom were to be employed in India or the colonies. But it is equally plausible, and much more in keeping with the expressed beliefs of some of the leading schoolmasters of the period, to regard the development as part of a deliberate campaign to win adherents to the teachings of the Church of England.

Evidence of this can be found in the writings and achievements of Nathaniel Woodard, founder of Lancing and Hurstpierpoint schools and one of the leading educational propagandists of his time. Woodard devised a scheme for Christian education in England with divisions into five regions and three grades. Schools in the top grade would educate the sons of gentlemen and professional men; those in the second grade the sons of superior tradesmen, semi-professional men and farmers; and those in the third the sons of small tradesmen and artisans. A provost was to be in charge of each region, Woodard himself undertaking to serve as provost for the south at Lancing.

'Somehow or other,' Woodard wrote, 'we must get possession of the Middle Classes, especially the lower section of them, and how can we so well do this as through Public Schools? . . . Education without religion is, in itself, a pure evil.' About half a million pounds were raised by public subscription in support of his educational plans.

It was in this spirit that other reformers and crusaders fought for the spiritual welfare of young readers of fiction. To their credit they did not do so by procuring a ban on penny dreadfuls. Instead they provided alternative forms of literature with the express intention of winning young readers from a kind of writing of which they disapproved to one which they considered healthy. Hence the appearance in 1867 of the magazine *Chatterbox*.

Sixty years later the diamond jubilee of *Chatterbox* was celebrated, and in an editorial on the history of the magazine it was stated:

> When CHATTERBOX was first founded, it was meant to provide something better for boys to read than what used to be called the 'penny dreadful'. . . . Such stories were never up to the mark unless a great deal of blood was shed. Ordinary laws and decent behaviour did not matter, so long as the hero killed all the villains. . . . It was thought, with pretty good grounds, that tales like this did much harm, by giving a false idea of life and setting wrong standards of reckless courage. It was said, and sometimes proved in the police courts, that boys became criminals through the wild love of excitement such stories bred in them. So CHATTERBOX and other magazines, of which few have survived, were started to provide *good* entertainment—plain, healthy stories in which the hero could have probable, enjoyable, gallant adventures without splashing blood on every page.

That the publishers of *Chatterbox* achieved their purpose, at least in part, was made clear by J. M. Barrie in the first printed edition of *Peter Pan*. As a boy, he revealed, he had not only bought penny dreadfuls and read them, though they were forbidden, but he had even tried to write them. Then the high–class magazine *Chatterbox* had touched his better nature, and he had borne secretly to the garden and buried not only the printed bloods but his own imitations of them. *Chatterbox,* he made it clear, had saved him.

The world may or may not owe Peter Pan in part to *Chatterbox*. What is certain is that a new popular medium was established in which young heroes of the kind portrayed by Ballantyne could proliferate through the efforts of more imitative and less gifted authors, and a new profile of the ideal of an English boy became familiar to young readers.

Chatterbox moreover was only one of a number of new magazines which sprang up to serve the same avowed purpose. An even more influential publication was the *Boy's Own Paper,* whose controlling body was the Religious Tract Society.

CHAPTER THREE

Schoolboy Story Heroes

The first number of the *Boy's Own Paper* was published on 18 January 1879. The first article was entitled *My First Football Match,* and, like *Tom Brown's School Days,* it was attributed simply to 'an Old Boy'. There followed a poem, whose opening stanza was:

> Whatever you are, be brave, boys!
> The liar's a coward and slave, boys!
> Though clever at ruses,
> And sharp at excuses,
> He's a speaking and pitiful knave, boys!

Next the Reverend J. G. Wood announced that he had responded to the editor's invitation to show what could be done in practical natural history with a jack-knife. 'I have been out with such a weapon,' he wrote, 'and have had a capital time of it.' He then called attention to the merits of that part of a jack-knife designed for picking stones out of horses' hooves.

After this came a short biography of the Afghan Dilawar Khan, who is described as a brigand but contrasted favourably with Hindus, who 'true to their instinct would commence haggling'.

Dilawar Khan meets Major Lumsden, 'one of those frank, brave soldiers of whom the north–west provinces of India have always had noble specimens, and whose personal influence makes a defence stronger far than armed forts and scientific frontiers'. Lumsden Sahib wins Dilawar Khan's heart at once, and during the Indian mutiny 'the manliness of Dilawar's bearing and his undoubted loyalty to the English made him a great favourite among the British officers of his regiment'. In time Dilawar Khan is impressed by 'the comparative (*sic*) purity of the life of Europeans, their honesty and love of justice'. This convinces him that Christianity is superior to Mohammedanism, and he is duly baptized in Peshawar.

The fifth item in the opening number was 'How I Swam the Channel' by Captain Webb. For his first attempt, the author explains, he did not consider the weather suitable, 'but people kept saying to me, "Look here, Webb; you must go. There are all these people down from town; and if you don't start they'll say it's all talk."'

With these first offerings a moral tone was set, a style was established, and a pattern for heroes was delineated, with all of which readers would grow increasingly familiar. Continuity was assisted by the fact that the first editor, G. A. Hutchinson, remained in office until 1913, and the popularity of the style and the contents was proved by the sales. After only four years the circulation of the *Boy's Own Paper* was about a quarter of a million.

The imprint of the publishers of the *Boy's Own Paper,* the Religious Tract Society, was evidently considered too forbidding for a magazine offering adventure stories for boys. The ostensible publishing house was therefore the 'Leisure Hour' office in Paternoster Row in the City of London. The committee of the Religious Tract Society occasionally expressed doubts about editorial policy, particularly about the high proportion of fiction and the lack of prominence given to 'Christian truth and influence'. But Hutchinson's touch was fairly sure, and like all good editors he had a talent for spotting the authors he wanted before they had achieved fame.

*   *   *

The anonymous author of the first article in the first number of the *Boy's Own Paper* was in fact Talbot Baines Reed, a writer whose influence on the development of the English school story, its ethics and its heroes, can hardly be overestimated. In a history of children's books, which was published in 1962, Marcus Crouch, summarizing books about boys' schools in the 1920s, made the point that there were no new significant developments and that the books still conformed to the pattern created by Talbot Baines Reed forty years earlier.

Reed was well fitted by heredity and upbringing to catch the spirit of the Religious Tract Society. His grandfather was a philanthropist who founded those badly needed though uncompromisingly named institutions, the Asylum for Idiots at Earlswood and the Hospital for Incurables at Putney. His father was an active member of the British and Foreign Bible Society, of which his elder brother, the Reverend Charles Reed, became secretary. Talbot Baines Reed was himself a deacon in the Congregational Church.

The activity for which his background might not have seemed altogether suitable was the creation of the public school of fiction, for Reed never attended a boarding school, nor was he at any time a schoolmaster. It could also be maintained that he was not a professional writer. This was certainly the view taken by his biographer, the eminent typographer, Stanley Morison, who chose as the sub-title of his biography of Reed *Author, Bibliographer, Typefounder.* Reed was an active partner in the successful family printing business; he spent ten years in research for his important work, *A History of the Old English Letter Foundries,* and so little was he concerned with writing for profit that he transferred the copyright of his novels about school life to the Religious Tract Society for a nominal sum. The anonymity which he chose for his contributions to the *Boy's Own Paper* was maintained in the numerous essays, book reviews and other articles which he wrote for the *Leeds Mercury*.

Reed wrote a number of short stories for the *Boy's Own Paper* about an imaginary school called Parkhurst, and Hutchinson then persuaded him to try writing a serial story about school life. The outcome was *The Adventures of a Three Guinea Watch*, forerunner of *The Fifth Form at St Dominic's* and *Tom, Dick and Harry*, works whose very titles have passed into the consciousness of many to whom the name of Talbot Baines Reed himself now means little.

The narrator of *The Adventures of a Three Guinea Watch* is the watch itself, which passes through the hands of various owners. The first of these, and the principal hero of the book, is Charlie Newcombe, who is introduced to us as 'a curly-haired, bright-eyed boy of thirteen with honest, open face, good features and winning smile'. He is then about to start his first term at Randlebury school. Charlie has two particular friends at school. One of these is Jim Halliday, whose character is most clearly portrayed after he has left Randlebury and gone up to Cambridge.

Jim Halliday—now a strapping youth of nineteen—was a good representative of the 'steady set' at St George's College. Indeed, as he was intending to become a clergyman in due time, it would have been a deplorable thing if this had not been the case. He worked hard, and though not a clever fellow, had already taken a good position in the examination lists of his college. He was also an ardent superintendent at a certain boys' club in the town conducted by University men.

In addition he was 'a good bat, a famous boxer, a desperate man in a football scrimmage, and a splendid oar'.

Both Charlie and Jim at different times become owners of the watch, and as the watch insists that Charlie is its favourite master, we may deduce that Charlie is a hero of no ordinary quality. The author makes it clear that this quality is not primarily intellectual. We find Charlie 'sitting in his study attempting, with many groans, to make sense out of a very obscure passage in Cicero'. He is weak at mathematics, and he does not go to a university, but instead makes the Army his career.

Charlie's other friend has the informative name of Tom Drift, and their friendship begins in a curious manner. In a train on his way to school for the first time Charlie meets a woman who expresses the hope that Charlie will be friends with her son, Tom Drift, at Randlebury. Charlie promises he will be, and this promise he considers binding in spite of all Tom's eccentricities of conduct.

Tom Drift has a variegated career. It is emphasized early on that he is not a wholly bad character, but he is easily led, and his downfall begins when he comes under the influence of Gus Burke, 'one of the smallest and most vicious boys at Randlebury'. Gus is the son of a country farmer, 'who had the unenviable distinction of being one of the hardest drinkers and fastest riders in his county'. Gus himself has 'at his tongue's tip all the slang of the stables and all the blackguardisms of the betting–ring'.

For no evident reason other than that of corrupting him Gus and his friends decide to lure Charlie to a race meeting, Tom Drift being used as a decoy. The occasion is a school holiday, which takes place every year on the anniversary of the death of an Old Randle-burian, who 'in a famous battle between her Majesty's troops and those of a hostile and savage king' saved the regimental colours by wrapping them round his body before dropping from his horse into his comrade's arms 'a dead man'.

On his way back from the race meeting Charlie finds himself 'in the midst of a yelling, blaspheming, drunken multitude, from the sight of whose faces and the sound of whose words his soul revolted'. A fight breaks out, and two older Randlebury boys who happen to be on the spot, 'broad–shouldered, tall fellows,' pitch in, whereupon 'a panic set in among the blackguards'.

Gus is expelled, but he is not finished yet. Tom Drift becomes a medical student on leaving school, and for a time he is sustained in the right course by Charlie's hearty, jolly letters and by regular visits to Charlie's parents. But temptation is never far away. Tom reads a 'trashy' novel; then his better nature asserts itself and he throws it into the fire, but the next day he goes out and buys another copy. He lingers in front of a 'low theatre', where one of Shakespeare's plays is being performed, fighting hard against his urge to go inside. Then Gus appears and drags him away to a music–hall. After that Tom goes steadily downhill, through pawnshops, in one of which the narrator watch stays for a time, to prison. Here he meets the Reverend Jim Halliday, now the owner of the watch and on temporary duty as prison chaplain. Jim successfully reminds Tom of better days by leaving the watch with him for a whole night. 'Tom Drift,' the watch records, 'turned and knelt, with me still clasped in his hands. And so that night, and with it the crisis of Tom Drift's life, was passed.'

The watch has one more important service to render. While soldiering in India during the period of the mutiny Charlie recovers the watch, and the night before going into battle he falls asleep like a child, 'whistling one of the old Randlebury songs'. The next day he is first into the breach in storming Lucknow and is thought by his comrades to have been shot through the heart. A surgeon then discovers that the bullet has been diverted by the watch. The surgeon is Tom Drift.

The Fifth Form at St Dominic's is in a number of respects a more satisfying work than *The Adventures of a Three Guinea Watch*. There is a similar plot involving the downfall and subsequent regeneration of a weak but not fundamentally vicious character, and once again the downhill progress is precipitated by drink and gambling. Reed repeatedly claimed that his kind of school story was altogether unlike *Eric or Little by Little*. In fact the similarity of some of the plots used by the two authors is evident. It is in the characters of the heroes that the most noticeable differences are to be found.

The counterpart of Tom Drift at St Dominic's is Edward Loman, who comes to the school relatively late in life from another school and never achieves popularity. Loman's decline starts when he finds himself in debt to the publican of the Cockchafer, whose name is Cripps. Some readers may think that Cripps shows remarkable forbearance before pressing for a settlement, but Reed, who had a distinct inclination, which is surprising in a Victorian novelist and was certainly not shared by Ballantyne, to equate morality with class, describes Cripps as 'not exactly a gentleman'. He 'frequently helped himself to an overdose of his own beverages, besides being a sharp hand at billiards, and possessing several packs of cards with extra aces in them'. The crunch comes when Cripps visits Randlebury school to watch a rugby football match, in which Loman plays so badly that he loses the respect of all his fellows.

> Had the captain and his men known the cause of all this —had they been aware that the flash, half–tipsy cad of a fellow who, with a dozen of his 'pals', was watching the match with a critical air, there at the ropes was the landlord of the Cockchafer himself, the holder of Loman's 'little bill' for £30, they would perhaps have understood and forgiven their comrade's clumsiness. But they did not.

Loman steals an examination paper from the headmaster's study and is expelled, but in the final chapter we learn that he has pulled himself together through four or five years' 'farming and knocking about in Australia'. Australia, indeed, offered an opportunity for regeneration in many Victorian works of fiction. A number of the hero–villains of penny dreadfuls were deported there in a manner which satisfied the demands of the law while retaining the sympathy of the reader; Charles Reade in his passionately didactic *It's Never Too Late to Mend* exploited the theme with memorable success.

Repetitive though its plot may be, there is nevertheless in *The Fifth Form at St Dominic's* an evocation of a school atmosphere which is convincing enough to make much of the book excellent reading. The complex forms of group and institutional loyalties, the contents of the school magazine, the sheer physical exuberance and noise of the boys in the lowest forms—all these are as authentic as the manner in which the various characters spend their holidays. Raleigh, the captain of the school, is to be found climbing Snowdon with his sisters; Bramble, the most unruly of the juniors, searches for crabs on the rocks at Broadstairs; the formidable headmaster, the 'Doctor', recoups his strength among the peaks and passes of Switzerland.

There is too some subtlety in the delineation of character. A partial hero, Oliver Greenfield, is an extremely clever boy, who wins two scholarships and who has an interesting form of pride. When it is generally believed that he, not Loman, stole the examination papers and he is sent to Coventry in consequence, he refuses to deny the charge. On being reproached for not doing so, he says:

> 'Posing as a martyr and a saint! no! I'd sooner pose as a coward than set up as a saint when I'm not one.'

Oliver's younger brother Stephen is a convincing and likable junior hero until he too nearly goes adrift through the wiles of Cripps; at that point a sudden access of priggishness is perhaps permissible. But the principal hero, Horace Wraysford, known as 'Wray', comes from the now familiar mould. 'A handsome, jovial-looking boy of sixteen . . . one of the best "all-round men" in the Fifth, or indeed in the school. He is certain to be in the School Eleven against the County, certain to win the mile race and the "hurdles" . . . and not at all unlikely to carry off the Nightingale Scholarship.' He does not win the scholarship, this distinction going to his cleverer and more complicated friend, Oliver Greenfield, but his true quality emerges when he saves the young Stephen Greenfield from drowning. (Students of Ballantyne might be pardoned for supposing that there is something derivative in Reed's use of the rescue–from–drowning theme. In fact Reed himself, at the age of seventeen, was awarded a medal by the Royal Humane Society for saving a cousin from drowning off the coast of Londonderry.) Wray also shows his mettle in a fight with the habitués of the Cockchafer, as do the Greenfield brothers. 'The contest was short and sharp. A pair of well–trained athletic schoolboys, with a plucky youngster to help them, are a match any day for twice the number of half-tipsy cads. . . . As for Loman, he had disappeared.'

The literary merits of *The Fifth Form at St Dominic's* are possibly underrated today. What of its moral merits? The editor of the *Boy's Own Paper* seems to have had no doubts. In a preface to the book he wrote:

> It is difficult to conceive any reader, be he young or old, who would not be the better for its vivid portraiture and bracing atmosphere. . . . The story forcefully illustrates how rapidly they may sink who once tamper, for seeming present advantage, with truth, and how surely, sooner or later, a noble character comes to vindication and honour, and in all such respects it is eminently true to life.

After pointing out that the boys depicted were neither angels nor monstrosities, Hutchinson added that they had 'that moral grit and downright honesty of purpose that are still, we believe, the distinguishing mark of the true British public-school boy'.

Why *public*-school boy, some latter-day readers may be inclined to ask. Perhaps more pertinently, why 'still'? Was the editor of the *Boy's Own Paper* concerned in the early 1880s that the moral standards accepted by one generation might be in jeopardy with the next? Very probably he was. The anxiety has been a familiar one through the ages.

In Reed's *The Master of the Shell* the principal hero is not a boy but a master. There is, it is true, a secondary hero, the captain of the house, Ainger, who is stamped with the familiar Talbot Baines Reed mark. He is 'steady as a rock at the wickets of the first eleven' and 'popular because he had won the mile, and was upright, and meant what he said, and said what he meant'. But the reader's sympathies are expected to be predominantly with the newly appointed master at Grandcourt school, Mark Railsford.

Railsford becomes engaged in the first chapter to a girl named Daisy, whom he meets while she is on holiday with her family in

Lucerne. Part of this family is her younger brother Arthur, a boy at Grandcourt school. The need to support a wife in the future induces Railsford to abandon the life of a 'gentleman at large', and he is duly appointed as a housemaster and master of the Shell. Among the qualifications which win him these appointments is a blue for rowing.

The relationship between Railsford and his future brother-in-law, the young boy in the Shell, or 'shellfish', Arthur Herapath, is skilfully depicted. On Arthur's side there is a mixture of hero-worship, proprietary pride, the desire to exploit a special relationship to advantage, and the perpetual, enormous joke that Railsford is 'spoons' about Arthur's sister and has even been overheard calling her 'Chuckey'. Arthur himself is also 'spoons' for a time about the Doctor's niece, Miss Violet, but his feelings find what is presumably thought to be their proper perspective in ridicule when he asks: 'How soon do fellows get enough money to marry?' Daisy and Violet have about as much flesh and blood as their names suggest.

The moral problem confronting Mark Railsford arises from a physical assault on Bickers, the unpopular master of the house next door, who is found tied up in a sack in a boot cupboard in Railsford's house. Railsford and Bickers have quarrelled, and Railsford is suspected by many of knowing who the assailant was and by some of being the culprit himself.

At the end of one term Railsford stays behind as a kind of duty officer, and a boy in Bickers's house, whose name is Branscombe, contracts diphtheria. While searching among Branscombe's papers for the address of the boys' parents Railsford finds a document, some of it in classical Greek, which readers are presumably expected to understand. This is a confession that Branscombe was the chief instigator of the assault on Bickers. In a state of delirium Branscombe shortly afterwards confirms his guilt.

It is in the use to be made of this knowledge that Railsford's dilemma lies.

What right had he—a man of honour and a gentleman—to

use it, even if by doing so he could redress one of the greatest grievances in Grandcourt? . . . After two terms of hard work and honest battle, was he to be turned away, cashiered and ruined, just because he had stayed to nurse a sick boy and over-heard his delirious confession? So the battle went on, and Railsford fought it out inch by inch, like a man. He was not single-handed in such matters: he had a Friend who always wins, and He helped Railsford to win that night.

A more mundane satisfaction is provided when Branscombe's father appears and explains what has happened—an act, it may be thought, of some generosity.

Talbot Baines Reed died of tuberculosis at the age of forty-one. In his short, varied and vigorous life he, in conjunction with the editor of the *Boy's Own Paper,* created a new moral standard for the school story, and with it a kind of hero who may not have been altogether new in conception, but who would impress his personality on schoolboy stories for decades to come. This hero, clearly Newbolt Man in embryo, seems to have had much in common with Reed himself. A friend who attended the same day school as Reed, the City of London school, described him as 'a handsome boy, strong and well proportioned, with a frank, open face, black hair, and lively dark eyes, fresh complexion, full of life and vigour, and with a clear ringing voice. . . . In football he was A I'. This evidently was Charlie Newcombe of Randlebury. The same boy would have found himself at home a decade or two later at Greyfriars school in the company of Harry Wharton and Bob Cherry.

Talbot Baines Reed and other contributors to the *Boy's Own Paper* wrote predominantly for middle or upper-middle-class readers who would, they assumed, have some knowledge of public-school life. In one of his novels Reed wrote: 'Then speech-day began. My readers hardly want me to describe so familiar a scene. . . . The reader knows all about it; he has been through it.' The *Boy's Own*

Paper advised its readers to take cold baths regularly, but was considerate enough to ask them not to splash about too much for the sake of the servants. (The bizarre practice of taking cold baths when hot water is available and can be afforded persisted in English popular literature for several decades. It is mentioned *en passant* that Mark Railsford is addicted to the habit; many of John Buchan's heroes can be relied upon to take a cold bath as surely as they can to rise to the top of their profession.) But whatever the intention of the earlier writers may have been, the avid, even compulsive reading of works of fiction purporting to describe life in an English public school eventually spread far beyond the middle classes. George Orwell in the 1930s recorded having seen a young coal-miner, who had already worked for a year or two underground, eagerly reading the *Gem,* and when he himself gave a batch of magazines to some Englishmen serving in the French Foreign Legion they picked out the *Gem* and the *Magnet* first. Presumably it was from such sources that these readers derived their knowledge of the English public school and of the stereotype of the hero which it produced.

In presenting heroes who consistently conformed to type, popular school stories may have reflected a tendency towards increased standardization in the public–school product himself. In 1912 Arthur Ponsonby, in his book *The Decline of the Aristocracy,* wrote that stereotyping was 'perhaps the strongest indictment that has to be brought against our Public Schools'. In illustration of this he contrasted group photographs taken at schools in the 1860s and 1870s, in which there had been considerable variety and individuality of appearance, with the general conformity to type in comparable photographs forty or fifty years later. It is also likely that Reed and his successors by their very popularity contributed to this standardization.

The claim that the influence of Talbot Baines Reed still pervaded schoolboy stories of the 1920s can be supported by an examination of the style and contents of many hundreds of works which are little remembered today. One such appeared in the *Chatterbox* annual for 1929, which, if only for economy in use of words and skill in narration, merited the popularity it enjoyed. This was 'The Strange Mystery of the Grey House' by Frances Cowen.

The hero is Tom Holland, 'fresh from Clifton, fourteen, and already in the cricket eleven'. He has twin sisters, Jackie and Jill, and their father, Colonel Holland, is 'a high official of one of the Indian States'. The parents are unable to come home for the school holidays as planned—'they've been having trouble with the natives out there'—and the children are due to stay with their Uncle Peter, whom they have never met. In fact they are lured to a grey house with a large garden by a man posing as Uncle Peter and by an Indian with a crooked body, and, needless to say, a crooked mind, who is in reality a prince but who is posing as Uncle Peter's servant.

Tom faces various dangers with a courage which inspires the girls, and after a time he decides to break out of the grounds, but he does not confide his plan to his sisters.

> Tom considered the twins not bad for girls, but girls, he had heard, were inclined to get excited and blurt things out, or to be panicky and miserable.

Once over the garden wall Tom runs into his friend Hardean, whose parents happen to own the house next door. Hardean is captain of the cricket eleven and 'something of a blood'. (Perhaps because the author is a woman the gulf dividing the captain of cricket from a fourteen–year–old boy, however gifted athletically, which Reed would have scrupulously respected, is here ignored.) Hardean has the good fortune to have a father who is 'a sport and something in the Foreign Office', and he himself is sagacious enough to suspect that Uncle Peter is probably an impostor.

> Tom stopped, struck by a sudden thought. 'His hands!' he exclaimed.
> 'What's the matter with them?'
> 'The finger–nails are bluish, like a half–breed's.'

Hardean nodded his head sagely. 'I told you so. The man isn't your uncle. He's probably a beastly dago.'

The real Uncle Peter eventually arrives in the grounds piloting a private aircraft. Tom 'could only see a wide clean shaven mouth and a row of white and regular teeth, but somehow he was reassured'.

In explaining how he discovered the house Uncle Peter gives most of the credit to the school cricket captain. 'A friend of yours, owning a great deal of common–sense and pluck, by the way, gentleman by the name of Hardean, has a father at the Foreign Office who happens to be an acquaintance of mine, same clubs and all that.' It also transpires that the purpose of the kidnapping is to put pressure on Colonel Holland in order that the crooked Indian can succeed his brother as maharajah.

Some of the variations from the Talbot Baines Reed original are immediately apparent. New technological devices such as aircraft are introduced, and the world of international intrigue is brought near to the life of the schoolboy. Some of the enemies to be fought are also new. Although the Indian mutiny did influence him significantly, as it did so many of his contemporaries, Reed was relatively indulgent to those who were not British. In *The Master of the Shell* there is a French master named M. Lablache. 'His backbone was limp, and he never did the right thing at the right time.' But he arouses our sympathies because in a tiny cottage in Boulogne he is keeping a paralyzed father and three motherless children, and this is why he 'clung to his unlovely calling of teaching unfeeling English boys at the rate of £30 a term'. The dust–ups in Reed's novels tend to be with cads and blackguards who frequent the local pubs; the iniquity of bluish finger–nails has not yet been discovered. The heroes, on the other hand, have barely altered. Hardean and Tom Holland would soon have settled down and made their marks at St Dominic's. Although their professions were somewhat different, Uncle Peter and Mark Railsford would instantly have recognized each other as kindred spirits.

There were, it is true, novelists writing in the late nineteenth and early twentieth centuries in England who chose public schools as the setting for novels, yet who succeeded in creating original and not stereotyped heroes. One such was Rudyard Kipling.

The critic George Sampson described Kipling's *Stalky & Co.* as 'an unpleasant book about unpleasant boys in an unpleasant school'. It could also less aphoristically be described as a memorable book by a writer of distinction about three exceptional boys in a school serving a small but clearly defined minority group. The school is the United Services College at Westward Ho!, which Kipling attended, and the book is dedicated to Cormell Price, who was headmaster in Kipling's time. Eighty per cent of the boys, it is stated in the book, were born abroad, 'in camp, cantonment, or upon the high seas'. Nearly all those we meet serve later in one capacity or another in India, most of them in the Army. The function of the school being what it was, the boy heroes might reasonably be expected to be impregnated, to some extent at least, with the Talbot Baines Reed ethos. In fact they escape it almost entirely.

In the very first paragraph of the book Stalky, M'Turk and Beetle are found smoking. Later they drink beer. King, their least favourite master, says of them: 'Of course they were drinking and smoking somewhere. That kind of boy always does. They think it manly.'

Beetle, who is a self-portrait of Kipling when young, is a poet and wears spectacles or 'gig-lamps'. ('The life of a poet at a big school is hard.') The literary tastes of all three are unorthodox: Stalky reads Surtees, Beetle Browning and M'Turk Ruskin. Their characters baffle their housemaster Prout, who describes them as 'unboylike, abnormal, and, in my opinion, unsound'. Prout also finds their tastes and interests heretical. He had 'heard M'Turk openly deride cricket—even house-matches; Beetle's views on the honour of the house he knew were incendiary; and he could never tell when the soft and smiling Stalky was laughing at him'.

One of the most successful exploits of Stalky and his two friends is to introduce a dead cat, which Stalky has shot, under the floor-boards in a dormitory in King's house as a counter-argument to the allegation that the boys in Prout's house dislike washing. Understandably none of the three becomes a prefect.

The regime is a harsh one. Kipling knew what bullying was, and he clearly enjoyed a vicarious revenge when describing how Stalky, Beetle and M'Turk reduce to 'scalding tears; appeals for mercy and abject promises of peace' two 'precocious hairy youths' of seventeen, who have themselves been guilty of bullying a fag. The three friends survive, indeed triumph over, the regime by guile, flexibility and Stalky's powers of leadership. 'Like many other leaders, Stalky did not dwell on past defeats.'

The head of the school, Carson, makes only a brief appearance towards the end of the book. He is described as 'a simple, straight-minded soul, and a pillar of the First Fifteen', who has a 'severely Philistine study'. The only master, apart from the head, whom Stalky and his friends respect is the Reverend John Gillett, who is fat and imperturbable and considered by his enemies to be 'a guileful Jesuit'. 'I don't talk about ethics and moral codes,' Gillett says, 'because I don't believe that the young of the human animal realises what they mean for some years to come.' Cormell Price, unlike most headmasters of the time, was not in holy orders, nor is the thinly disguised headmaster in the book, a fact on which Stalky comments approvingly.

Almost the worst moments which Stalky and his friends endure come when a Conservative Member of Parliament gives a talk on patriotism and shakes the Union Jack in front of the assembled school. To Stalky he is the 'Jelly–bellied Flag–flapper'. M'Turk sums him up before hearing him speak. 'He looks a bit of a bargee', he says. M'Turk has heard the M.P. arguing with the driver about his fare.

In the final chapter, with Beetle now writing in the first person, we learn how some of the principal characters have fared after leaving school.

'Stalky is the great man of his Century,' said Dick Four.

'How d'you know?' I asked.

'How do I know?' said Dick Four scornfully. 'If you've ever been in a tight place with Stalky you wouldn't ask.'

Stalky is still the same superb improviser and tactician with the same contempt for established authority, able now to make puns in Pushtu. Beetle concludes: 'India's full of Stalkies—Cheltenham and Haileybury and Marlborough chaps—that we don't know anything about, and the surprises will begin when there is really a big row on.'

Adult Newbolt Man, it may be thought, has arrived in a new and convincing form, but in embryo he was not presented to us in the manner expected. Kipling too gives the lesser examples of the species a new dimension, that of the inarticulate. Another old boy from the United Services College known as Tertius tries to describe the scene:

'We got into a mess up the Khye-Kheen Hills a couple o' years ago, and Stalky pulled us through. That's all.'

M'Turk gazed at Tertius with all an Irishman's contempt for the tongue-tied Saxon.

'Heavens!' he said. 'And it's you and your likes govern Ireland.'

(The English—ah, the English!—they are quite a race apart.
Being void of self-expression they confide their views to none;
But sometimes in a smoking-room one learns how things were done.
Yes, sometimes in a smoking-room, through clouds of 'Ers' and 'Ums',
Obliquely and by inference illumination comes,
On some step that they have taken, or some action they approve,
Embellished with the *argot* of the Upper Fourth Remove.)

In 1903 a book appeared by a very young writer entitled *A Pre-*

fect's Uncle, which on the surface seems to be a wholly conventional school story. The school is named Beckford, and it 'gauged a fellow's character principally by his abilities in the cricket and football fields'. Except in the final tenth of the book, which is devoted to the winter term and, therefore, to rugby football, the boys seem to do very little other than play cricket. There is a head of a house named Gethryn and a captain of cricket named Norris, who have a bit of a difference, which they finally settle in a combined move as centre three-quarters. There are also the usual momentarily disturbing incidents of theft and cheating. But there is at least one interesting character who is enough of an original to seem somewhat incongrous in the all too familiar setting—so much so that he disappears half way through the book. This is Farnie, a fourteen-year-old boy, who is the uncle of Gethryn, the head of the house. Farnie 'looked as if he had seen the hollowness of things, for his face wore a bored, supercilious look'. Before coming to Beckford, he has been to three public schools, from two of which he was expelled. He is a match in wits for all his elders, it is he who commits the theft, and he also frequents a pub. Here his preferences are made clear, for he has a choice of playing ping-pong or billiards.

He was no pinger. Nor was he a pongster. But for billiards he had a decided taste. . . . It appeared likely that he would have the choice of three professions open to him, namely, professional billiard player, billiard marker, and billiard sharp. At each of the three he showed distinct promise.

The language of course betrays the author, as it does elsewhere. (' "I can always bowl like blazes after lunch," said the fast man to Pringle. "It's the lobster salad that does it, I think." ') Fifty years later P. G. Wodehouse was to publish another of his numerous books about life in a public school. Two changes have occurred. The school is called Wrykyn instead of Beckford, and there are now references to the possible crime of dropping May or Sheppard in the slips before they have scored. Fifty years earlier the names were Jessup and Palairet. Otherwise everything is much the same.

The masters all speak a stilted, pedantic English suggestive of a formidable elderly relation of Bertie Wooster; the professional cricketer refers to the young whom he has coached as 'Master' Joe and 'Master' Mike; the M.C.C. wicket-keeper takes off his gloves and proceeds to capture several wickets by bowling lobs (*sic*); the lunch-time score in a match played away is conveyed to the school by telegram; and a boy who is found reading *The Iron Pirate* considers it 'the last word in hot stuff'. (Max Pemberton, the author of *The Iron Pirate,* was in fact the first editor of *Chums.*) Nor is there any difference in the moral conveyed. A certain amount of family loyalty is displayed, and there is a general resolve that the school or the house shall win any contest in which it is engaged, but the playing-fields of Wrykyn, like those of Beckford, do little else to mould the characters of the boys. No other figure emerges who is quite so engaging as Farnie, but he has a rival in the later book in a boy named Wyatt, who climbs out of his dormitory window every night of term. It is to be assumed that, as in the Wodehouse world generally, the weather was always fine.

Kipling and Wodehouse, being writers of unusual distinction, were able to command large sales from books whose boy heroes did not conform to a standard pattern. For the less gifted, or the less original, the safe formula for success remained, far into the twentieth century, strict orthodoxy in the choice of hero, though variety was permissible in the other characters. Nothing illustrates this more clearly than the literary career of Charles Hamilton *alias* Frank Richards, whose other pen-names included Martin Clifford, Owen Conquest, Hilda Richards, Clive Clifford and Ralph Redway.

The output of Frank Richards, the name by which he preferred to be known, was prodigious. At one stage he was writing the entire contents of two weekly magazines, *Gem* and *Magnet.* There was also a plan for the production of a French magazine featuring a French school with a French hero named Raoul, which Richards was to write in its entirety in French himself, a task he would have faced with equanimity. Regrettably this plan was never put into effect.

Richards's success as a writer was both immediate and continuous. In his autobiography, which was written in the third person, he stated: 'People have sometimes asked him about his "early struggles". But he never had any. . . . Everything started well, and went on well.' He was too the creator of a schoolboy who seems more certain of immortality than any other in English fiction, Billy Bunter. But for schoolboy heroes Richards knew what his readers wanted, and he had no hesitation in giving it to them.

> Boys love an exciting story [he wrote] and why should they not? And if they cannot get a clean and wholesome one they will take what they can get. . . . The average healthy boy really would rather see his hero at the wicket, or speeding along the touchline with the ball at his feet, or even perpetrating a 'howler' under the gimlet-eye of his form-master, than handling deadly weapons and shedding oceans of blood.

So he gave the world Harry Wharton, acknowledged leader of the Famous Five at Greyfriars school, whom he described in verse:

> He's a most obstinate fellow—
> A boy of the old soldier's breed—
> Let Bolsover growl and Bull bellow,
> Harry Wharton will still keep the lead.
> He's learnt to control a quick passion,
> Yet he knows how to use a quick fist—
> He can deal, in most summary fashion,
> With a foe, yet knows when to desist!
> Harry Wharton—to put it in short—
> Is the best of all types—a good Sport!

Tom Merry is his counterpart at St Jim's:

> You get a boy that's full of grit,
> Tom Merry—kindest of the kind!

And yet—he's shown it oft and oft—
The very opposite of soft.

Three of Harry Wharton's associates in the Famous Five at Grey-friars differ from their leader in little except physical characteristics. The fifth is Hurree Ramset Jam Singh, known to his friends as Inky. Inky speaks a highly idiosyncratic babu English, but because of his liking for cricket he is probably in some way derived from Prince Ranjitsinhji. Richards wrote of this character: 'By making an Indian boy a comrade on equal terms with English schoolboys, Frank felt he was contributing a mite towards the unity of the Common-wealth, and helping to rid the youthful mind of colour prejudice.' No doubt he meant it. The Jewish boy, Montague Rowland, is also relatively popular, in spite of the inordinate wealth of his uncle Isaac, and Wun Lung, the Chinese, though inevitably rather crafty, adapts himself pretty well to English school life.

The masters are little more than symbols of authority. Henry Samuel Quelch, M.A., in whose form the Famous Five, Billy Bunter and others remain in perpetuity, is distinguishable from his col-leagues mainly by his gimlet-eye. But the old boys are a significant lot. Quelch himself in his *History of Greyfriars* records that 'among its Old Boys the school can boast a Cabinet Minister, a Major-General, a famous explorer, several County cricketers, and a news-paper proprietor'.

Throughout the Frank Richards schools a moral code is accepted, by the heroes in the observance and by others in the breach, which is a reflection of a common outlook on life. George Orwell witheringly described the outlook as that of 'a rather exceptionally stupid member of the Navy League in 1910'. Herbert Vernon-Smith, known as the Bounder, who sinks so low as to keep his hands continually in his pockets, is one of the readiest to use the familiar Richards phrase, 'fair play's a jewel'. Billy Bunter may be untruthful, have a mind revolving around cake, and find it difficult to distinguish between *meum* and *tuum*. He may be—and indeed is—called by Bob Cherry 'a funky rotter'. But his sins are essentially little more than gluttony and sloth. For heroes and dubious characters alike all problems of sex are disposed of by being ignored.

The *Gem* and the *Magnet* survived until 1939 and 1940 respectively, and even then paper shortage was the principal cause of their death. When the Billy Bunter books were published anew after the end of the war of 1939-45 they became extremely popular. They still are. But during the years in which the pupils of Greyfriars and St Jim's remained unaltered in age, intelligence, athletic ability, moral outlook and even idiom, some important new developments were taking place elsewhere in the school story. Among these was the writing of novels about school life which were intended for adult as much as for boy readers. One such was Ernest Raymond's *Tell England*.

There is plenty of cricket here too. Edgar Gray Doe, one of the two principal heroes, is an orphan living with his uncle, Sir Peter Gray, 'the once–famous Surrey bowler'. The junior housemaster, whom both Doe and the narrator, Rupert Ray, greatly admire, is S.T. Radley, 'the finest bat in the Middlesex team'. From time to time Radley delivers moral homilies which are in direct line of descent from the Religious Tract Society.

'Have I ever bullied you at the nets,' he said, 'for stepping back to a straight ball?'

'Yes, sir.'

'Well, the universal habit of "stepping back" is exactly parallel to that of arguing with conscience. The habit grows; one's wicket always falls after a few straight balls.'

Radley even quotes with approval Adam Lindsay Gordon's well known lines about life being mostly froth and bubble.

Doe and Ray and their friend Pennybet, however, leave school while the book still has much of its course to run. On leaving they do not simply become old boys. They are participants in a war in which the heroes of one's own side are liable to be killed, and their schoolboy morality then sustains them only up to a point.

The evil that we saw in the world and the army smashed our allegiance to the old moral codes. . . . We ceased to think there was any harm in being occasionally 'blotto' at night, or in employing the picturesque army word 'bloody'. Worse than that, we began to believe that vicious things, which in our boyhood had been very secret sins, were universally committed and bragged about.

After that it was 'an easy step, lightly taken, to the things of the night'.

Happily, once they are aboard a troopship Doe and Ray come under the influence of Padre Monty, who is determined to convince them that 'the old Church of England' has everything that public schoolboys need. He succeeds of course, some assistance being afforded by an occasional game of deck-tennis between early morning mass and breakfast. He even wins the two young subalterns over to the practice of confession, pointing out that if they have gone the whole way with their sins—whatever that may mean—'it's up to a sportsman to go the whole way with his confessions'.

However many doubts they may have had themselves, Doe and Ray, we feel, enter the Gallipoli campaign as innocent as they had been at school, when Ray loved Doe as Orestes loved Pylades and Doe liked Radley better than anyone else in the world and 'simply loved being whacked by him'. With sureness of judgment Ernest Raymond has both Doe and Ray, as well as their more sophisticated friend Pennybet, killed by the end of the book, and only an exceptionally insensitive reader is likely to remain dry-eyed throughout the account of Doe's death.

The war of 1914-18 served as a watershed affecting popular literature of many kinds, the school story being one of them. After the war was over the flow of conventional school stories continued unabated at a certain artistic level. But there was also a new stream of books, in which serious attempts were made to treat the problems of adolescence as they arise within the restrictive bounds of English public schools. Of these Alec Waugh's *The Loom of Youth,* published in 1917, was one of the earliest and most celebrated. *Tell England*, for all the traditionalism of its message and of the characters of the finest bat in the Middlesex team and of the Army padre, was a pointer in the direction of the new stream.

Contributors to the publications of the Religious Tract Society created the kind of world which they thought ought to exist, one in which right, as they saw it, always triumphed. His preface to *The Fifth Form at St Dominic's* suggests that the editor of the *Boy's Own Paper* believed the real world was not greatly different. The most prolific progeny of this line of writers, Frank Richards, by contrast, created a world of fantasy, and as not infrequently happens, it is the fantasy world which seems likeliest to survive.

For more than half a century these writers of conventional public school stories, both of the earnest and the fantastic varieties, continued to proclaim their message, and in doing so they conveyed to countless boys and girls a certain picture of what a public school was and ought to be, and of how those who attended them were expected to behave. The influence they exerted in the process was both incalculable and immense. Meanwhile other writers who were no less popular, and who also created English boy heroes, were helping to form a new impression of the history of the world, in particular of those parts in which British subjects served or conquered overseas.

CHAPTER FOUR

Boy Heroes and Imperial History

There is a widespread assumption that at some period in the past, which is usually unspecified, school–children in Britain were firmly encouraged by the way in which history was taught to believe in the merits of the British Empire as an institution and to consider it important and desirable that as many parts of the map of the world as possible should be coloured red. This is largely a delusion. In practice teachers have had a traditional reluctance to include within the scope of history anything which happened in the preceding thirty or forty years, and for this reason alone the teaching of imperial history was usually pretty meagre. There was also a shortage of textbooks which could serve to promote the imperialist message.

J. R. Green's *A Short History of the English People* was long regarded as a standard work and was widely used, sometimes in the original, sometimes in paraphrase or digest, for teaching history to the young. Green died in 1883, but his *Short History* was considered sufficiently important for the tale it told to be brought up to date by succeeding scholars. The Everyman edition of the *Short History,* published in 1960, runs to nearly 900 closely printed pages. In these Australia and New Zealand are mentioned only in passing in a brief summary of the events of the war of 1939-45. Singapore, Hong Kong and Gibraltar receive similar treatment. Canada after 1815 is accorded about a page, most of it devoted to the merits of the Durham report advocating self–government for the colonists. The immediate cause of the outbreak of the Indian Mutiny, the smearing of cartridges with the fat of cows and pigs, is described as 'gross tactlessness', and in the treatment of the South African war Dr Jameson and Cecil Rhodes appear as the principal miscreants. The whole concept of imperialism is largely disposed of in the sentence: 'In 1903 Mr Chamberlain, after his return from South Africa, advocated Colonial Preference as a means of welding together the several parts of the Empire.' The entire work in fact barely provides material for a single lesson on the benefits of imperialism.

There has, happily, never been an official political line for the teaching of history in schools in Britain, but in so far as a generally acceptable line can be discerned, Green was certainly influential in shaping it. In 1889 a book was published by J. G. Fitch, H. M. Inspector of Training Colleges, consisting of a series of lectures on teaching which he had delivered nine years earlier at Cambridge University. Through the teaching of history, he stated, 'every boy should be made to feel that unbought services will be required of him as member of parliament, magistrate, guardian or trustee, and that it will be honourable to render them'. The need for lessons on such subjects as public trusts, juries and municipal corporations is stressed, but of patriotism no more is said than that the aim should be to instill 'a rational and affectionate regard for the country in which we have been born, and for the privileges we enjoy in it'.

In history books written for younger children a similar restraint is to be found. In 1923 Blackie and Son published Book VI in a highly successful illustrated series dealing with history from 1688 onwards. Book VI is specifically concerned with relations with countries overseas. In it we learn that 'nothing can excuse the cruelty and wickedness' of Warren Hastings in 'wringing these large sums from almost helpless native governments', and that Pitt knew that 'while the Irish Protestants held power over there, the Roman Catholics would not have fair play'.

Advocates of imperialism indeed complained frequently and, from their point of view, justifiably of the neglect of the British Empire in the teaching of history in schools, but for a long time relatively little was done to reverse the trend by producing works which could be accepted as standard history text-books. H. Wood Jarvis did, it is true, launch a counter-attack in *Let the Great Story be Told.* Here we are presented with a picture of a British Empire which has been brought into being largely by a certain kind of character with whom readers must have become familiar through works of fiction. There is, for instance, John Smith of Virginia ('What name could have been more appropriate for the founder of the British Commonwealth of Nations than plain John Smith?') Smith's features were 'handsome and regular, and there was a slight hint of an inner well-spring of laughter in the keen, determined eyes'. An early missionary in New Zealand, the Reverend Samuel Marsden, is 'a sturdy Yorkshire parson of between forty-five and fifty years of age, whose arresting features showed an unusual blend of strength and gentleness'. Then there is Sir Thomas Roe, first English ambassador to the court of the Great Mogul, who on coming to present his credentials found some of the Mogul's officers 'lolling'. 'Something about his manner showed them that they were dealing with a man with whom it would be unwise to trifle. With one accord they rose to their feet, and their attitude of insolence changed to one of courtesy.' The counter-attack, however, came rather late. Wood Jarvis's book was written during the war of 1939–45. It was published in 1947, by which time the process of voluntarily dismantling the British Empire had already begun.

It is of course true that in the 1880s a sense of an imperial mission was spreading more and more widely among people in Britain. In a leading article published in the *National Observer* in August 1891 entitled 'A Great Idea', W. E. Henley wrote:

A few years ago Imperial Federation was but a zealot's dream, the fantastic creation of a mind run wild in patriotism. Now, though not within the region of practical politics, the subject is found worthy of a place in quarterly reviews.

By then the process of making young readers vividly aware, not only of the existence of an empire, but of how it came into being and of the kind of man believed to have created it and to be serving it, had already begun. But the works through which this was done were not the text-books of schools. They were, on the one hand, a new kind of popular journalism, and on the other a new school of historical fiction. The most powerful figure in the new journalism was Alfred Harmsworth. The most persuasive writer of the new historical fiction was George Alfred Henty.

Henty, on coming down from Cambridge, deliberately chose a life of adventure. This he began by combining the roles of soldier and war correspondent, much as Winston Churchill was to do later. Of his decision to join the Army, G. Manville Fenn, who published a scrappy but sympathetic biography of Henty, wrote: 'The Crimean war was on, and he too, strung up by that natural instinct that has made "Englishman" a name famous in the world's history, grew more and more restless.' Fenn was a personal friend and a journalistic colleague, whom Henty regarded highly.

Henty suffered much from illness in childhood, spending long periods in bed, when he read hugely. On leaving Westminster school, feeling perhaps the need to overcome natural weaknesses, he hired a well-known boxer and Cumberland-style wrestler to give him instruction. This seems to have proved useful in later life, particularly when he was a foreman in charge of a gang building a small military railway. One man, who had been fired for insubordination, continued to be abusive, and, in Fenn's words, 'Henty meantime was quietly taking off his coat and rolling up his sleeves preparatory to showing the unbelieving ruffian how a muscular athletic English gentleman . . . could scientifically handle his fists and give the scoundrel, to the intense delight of the lookers on, a thoroughly solid and manly thrashing'.

As a correspondent Henty spent some time with Garibaldi's legions and was present at the battle of Lissa in the Adriatic. He took part in the march on Magdala, when, to quote Fenn again, 'patient Britain . . . could no longer suffer the mocking insolence of the defiant ignorant ruler King Theodore of Abyssinia; and Sir Robert Napier was preparing his forces for the invasion of that comparatively unknown and warlike land'. He was in Paris in the days of the Commune following the French defeat in the Franco–Prussian war. He was nearly shipwrecked when aboard H. M. Stanley's launch off the west coast of Africa. He covered the Ashanti war of 1874, the Carlist war in Spain and the Turco-Serbian war. From this richness of experience he drew up a list of the principal requirements of a foreign correspondent. These were

that he should be a man capable of supporting hardships and fatigues; that he should possess a certain amount of pluck, a good seat in the saddle such as would enable him to manage any mount whose services he could command; and lastly, that he should have the manners of a gentleman and the knack of getting on well with all sorts and conditions of men.

All these qualities Henty himself possessed. Of his beliefs his biographer wrote:

Henty was a man of very strong political feeling, and possessed all the firm attributes of a thoroughly staunch Conservative gentleman, one might say Tory, of the past. If he had taken a motto, his would have been that of the old *John Bull* newspaper: 'God, the Sovereign, and the People'. Throughout his life, though gentle and kindly by nature, he was, when roused, by what he looked upon as injustice or cowardice, a fierce and truculent Briton, ready to defy the whole world.

Many of Henty's boy heroes would, one feels, become just such characters by the time they reached middle age.

As a foreign correspondent Henty seems to have been extremely conscientious, his reputation being that of a scrupulous recorder of facts. As a novelist, an occupation he took to relatively late in life, he adopted an unusual method, which must throw some doubt on the extent to which he was the true author of the works attributed to him.

Through their membership of the London Rowing Club Henty met J. P. Griffith, whom he employed, to use his own term, as an amanuensis, but whom some might consider a collaborator. Of their method of working Henty stated: 'I do not write any of my books myself. I get a man to do them for me—an amanuensis, of course; it all comes out of my head, but he does all the actual writing. I never see any of my work until it comes to me from the printers in the form of proof sheets.' The normal procedure was for Griffith to arrive at Henty's house at 9.30 a.m. and to stay for about four hours. He would return in the evening for about two hours, and in the course of such a working day they could expect to produce about 6,000 words, Griffith sitting at a table and Henty either sitting near him or lying on a sofa and pouring forth words. In this way nearly a hundred books were produced, from which countless boys probably learnt, or at least remembered, more about history in general, and that of the British Empire in particular, than they did from formal school lessons.

Henty—or Henty and Griffith—ranged fairly widely over history, but it is in the narration of deeds that won the empire that the characteristic Henty stamp is most evident. Few, if any, of his books attained more fame and popularity than *With Clive in India, or the Beginnings of an Empire*. The hero of this is Charlie Marryat, son of a Coastguard officer in Yarmouth.

His schoolfellows knew that Charlie Marryat's muscles were as firm and hard as those of any boy in the school. . . . When he was one of the hares there was but little chance for the hounds. He was a capital swimmer and one of the best boxers in the school. He had a reputation for being a leader in every mischievous prank; but he was honourable and manly, would scorn to shelter under the semblance of a lie, and was a prime favourite with his masters as well as with his schoolfellows.

Ballantyne or Reed could equally have sired Charlie Marryat, but this is history, and soon we shall be encountering Robert Clive himself.

Clive is presented as a complex character, described variously as gloomy, discontented, restless and queer, and hating his work as a clerk in the East India Company so much that he even tried to blow his brains out. Whereas Admiral Watson is said to have 'the punctilious sense of honour which naturally belongs to an English gentleman, Clive was wholly unscrupulous as to the means which he employed to gain his ends'.

English administration is not shown as wholly beneficent. A clerk named Johnson, complaining of living conditions in Madras, says: '"Our chiefs think of nothing but trade, and care nothing how squalid and miserable is the place in which they make their money."' The French, by contrast, who had occupied Madras earlier, had had larger ideas, 'forbad the natives to throw all their offal and rubbish on the beach, and made, in fact, a decent place of it'. When Calcutta is threatened Governor Drake and Captain Minchin, who is in command of troops, are both guilty of cowardice and dereliction of duty and escape by ship, leaving women and children behind. But of the general superiority of the British to the Indians little doubt is entertained, and of the integrity and heroism of Charlie Marryat none at all. Impressed by the riches of Trichinopoli, Charlie says: 'If these fellows could but fight as well as they work, and were but united among themselves, not only should we be unable to set foot in India, but the emperor, with the enormous armies which he would be able to raise, would be able to threaten Europe.' Later, when he is more experienced in the life of the country, he explains to his servant Tim: ' "It makes all the difference in the world with Indians. Let them attack you and they'll fight bravely enough. Go right at them and they're done for." '

Already on the voyage out to India Charlie distinguishes himself in a 'brush' with privateers and leaps overboard to save a man from drowning. In the various sieges and battles, which Henty describes with evident professional skill, he conducts himself admirably, and he has the gift of inspiring loyalty in those he commands. The man he saves from drowning, Tim Kelly, becomes his devoted and, because he is Irish, slightly comic servant for life, and there is also a dedicated Indian servant Hossein, who saves Charlie from starvation in the Black Hole of Calcutta and from destruction by a man–eating tiger. 'Between Hossein and Tim there was a sort of brotherly attachment, arising from their mutual love of their master.'

Charlie has a friend, Peters, to whom he says of his sister Kate: 'She would do nicely for you, Peters, when you go back. It would be awfully jolly if you two were to fall in love with each other.' A leading merchant named Haines, as he is dying, commends his daughter Ada to Charlie's care, and on their return to England Peters marries Kate and Charlie marries Ada. Tim also gets married and settles down in a house on Charlie's estate, doing no work but insisting till the end of his life that he is in Colonel Marryat's service. Finally, not to be outdone, Hossein, 'to the great amusement of his master and mistress, followed Tim's example. The pretty cook of Charlie's establishment made no objection to his swarthy hue.'

All this marriage business is confined to the final page of the book. In one of his earlier novels Henty made a boy of twelve kiss a girl of eleven. This elicited an indignant letter from a dissenting minister, and he did not make the same mistake again. 'I never touch on love interest,' he declared decisively.

When the action of the novel takes place overseas there is no question of where the sympathies of Henty's readers are expected to lie. The superiority of the British is established not only by upbringing and background but in some instances genetically. In *At the Point of the Bayonet: A Tale of the Mahratta War*, Harry Lindsay, after the murder of his parents, is brought up as an Indian. He is stronger than his companions and is their acknowledged leader. When Harry announces that he is English, Bajee Rao concedes that he has already noticed his energy, resourcefulness and readiness to accept responsibility. It is only when the fighting is on the home front that problems of partisanship are likely to arise. Henty was able to solve them by a skilful blend of sympathy with the romantic cause and unambiguous statements about where Britain's true interests lay.

In his preface to *Bonnie Prince Charlie: A Tale of Fontenoy and Culloden,* Henty wrote: 'It would have been far better for Prince Charlie's memory had he gained his wish and died at the head of his gallant Highlanders at Culloden.' Although there were few episodes in history more romantic than the Young Pretender's attempt to gain the throne, he went on, it was fortunate for Britain that the enterprise failed. Nevertheless the hero of the book is the young Ronald Leslie, whose father has taken service with the King of France and has secretly married a French heiress. The father, Colonel Leslie, incurs Louis XIV's displeasure, and he is imprisoned and his wife shut up in a convent. Ronald goes to France, and after various adventures and with the help of Marshal Saxe, under whom he has served at Fontenoy, he manages to rescue both his parents. Later Ronald serves the Young Pretender until the final disaster at Culloden.

Ronald is still a boy in the early stages of the book. We learn how, with another boy, he played truant and instead of going to school put out in a fishing boat and was unable to return home until the next day; how he played tricks on his dominie; but also how he conquered in single combat the son of Councillor Duff, the butcher, who had spoken disparagingly of the Stuarts. When Colonel Leslie's faithful old servant and trooper, who helps to bring Ronald up, meets Ronald's mother, he says: 'He is a right proper young gentleman, madam. Straight and comely and tall, with brown waving hair and a bright pleasant face. A son such as any mother might be proud of.' Lord George Murray takes a strong liking to Ronald when they campaign together, finding that his whole soul is in his work and that he cares nothing for 'the courtly gatherings around the person of the prince'.

In the end, in spite of their earlier allegiances, Ronald succeeds his father as Leslie of Glenlyon. Before that he has—*en passant,* so to speak—married the daughter of a neighbouring gentleman.

Scotland accepted the defeat as final, and the union between the two countries became close and complete. Henceforth Scotchmen went no longer to fight in the armies of France, but took service in that of their own country, and more than one of Ronald's grandsons fought stoutly in Spain under Wellington.

Flora Macdonald has been disposed of in less than a page.

With so many splendid boys growing into splendid young men, having adventures in different continents and different centuries, and ending up both happy and prosperous, it is not surprising that large numbers of young people in Britain gained a high proportion of their historical knowledge through the works of Henty. It was a big responsibility that he and Griffith carried, and one which they accepted with gusto. If the evidence of the number of reprints is to be relied on, the popularity of Henty's books, and therefore presumably their influence on the interpretation of history, was still little diminished in the 1920s.

Henty of course had his competitors. One who enjoyed considerable popularity for a time was W. H. G. Kingston. As a storyteller Kingston lacked something of Henty's easy flow, but as a propagandist for empire he was more deeply committed than Henty ever was, being editor of *The Colonist* and author of a manual entitled *How to Emigrate*. In his works of fiction Kingston wrote repeatedly of shipwreck, his geographical coverage of the subject being enormous. To the natural hazards which Kingston's heroes face are added those arising from the characters of the natives or 'savages', which with minimal exceptions are bloodthirsty and baleful.

Among the many perils [Kingston wrote] to which seamen are exposed must be reckoned that from the treachery of the savage inhabitants of some of the far distant lands which they visit. This was formerly greater than now, since the Missionary of the Gospel has gone forth with the Message of Peace, and been the means of bringing many of the fiercest tribes within the pale of civilization. The inhabitants of New Zealand were when first visited by Cook, and till long afterwards, the most savage, bloodthirsty, and vindictive people on the face of the earth, with the exception, perhaps, of the Fijians.

A vast number of young readers must, presumably, have believed this sort of comment and also similar statements about the inhabitants of the Andaman Islands, the Sandwich Islands and other remote places visited by such characters as the young Peter Trawl, who has a colourful record of survival from shipwreck. Unlike the typical Henty hero Peter Trawl is of humble origin, his parents having operated a bumboat off Portsmouth. But, as he himself says, 'it isn't so much what a man is born to which signifies, as what he becomes by his honesty, steadiness, perseverance, and above all by his earnest desire to do right in the sight of God'.

There may seem something incongruous in the way in which Kingston combined his pen–portraits of the inhabitants of distant territories with his advocacy of settlement among them, but the incongruity is perhaps more apparent in an age aware of the requirements of tourism than it was in one conscious of a need for missionaries. The absurdity of much of what he wrote became evident only with the advent of the relatively exact science of anthropology.

There were, too, numerous writers in direct line of descent from Henty, and even his style of title served others as a reliable formula for success. Captain F. S. Brereton, for instance, carried readers through much of the war of 1914-18 with books bearing such titles as *Under Haig in Flanders* and *With the Allies to the Rhine*. To Percy F. Westerman, who wrote more than 150 books for boys and who first became popular with a novel entitled, appropriately, *A Lad of Grit,* the Henty blueprint was also valuable. In Westerman's *The Young Cavalier: A Story of the Civil Wars* the problems of loyalty are comparable with those arising in

Henty's story of Ronald Leslie. Westerman's hero and narrator is Humphrey Markham, who at fifteen is 'tall and strong as many a lad of nineteen' and who has been brought up at his father's 'castle of Ashley, which lies betwixt the borders of Hamptonshire and Sussex, hard by the town of Petersfield'. By the time he is seventeen Humphrey is able to record:

> Thanks to clean–living and plenty of exercise in martial and open–air pursuits, I was strong, muscular, and active, yet withal (though I say it) I was of sound judgment, quick to act, and blessed with no small stock of intelligence.

Humphrey supports the royalist cause, and a footnote serves to explain that his narrative 'deals with the Civil War from the standpoint of a young Royalist'. When Ashley Castle is besieged, Humphrey records: 'In spite of the fact that they were our foes, I realised that they were Englishmen—and Englishmen of the good old fighting stock.' For the rest, we have Newbury and Lostwithiel and Carisbrooke Castle and other familiar place–names. Apart from Humphrey's mother the only woman to play any part in the events is the wife of a Devon sergeant. She is called, predictably, Mistress Widdicombe, and she is 'middle–aged, with calm, sweet–natured features'. She also has linen frills and ruffs which are 'white as snow'. Her function is to nurse Humphrey, who bears a strong physical resemblance to her son, back to health after a war injury. In short, another painless history lesson was provided, which could serve as a Christmas present easily chosen by thousands and readily accepted by thousands. The book was published in 1935, thirty–three years after Henty's death.

There were, it is true, historical novelists writing in the 1880s who commanded a wide following by relating the adventures of flesh–and–blood boy heroes, with whom we sympathize because we know they are nobody's carbon copies. There are few things more rewarding in Robert Louis Stevenson's works than his treatment of the relationship between David Balfour and Alan Breck in

Kidnapped: the boy from 'an ancient, honest, reputable house, peradventure in these latter days decayed', who has had a fairly simple country upbringing, and the proud, penniless, vain, quarrelsome Highland gentleman, poet and musician. ('Oh, man, am I no a bonny fighter?') After Alan has lost virtually everything he possesses at cards to Cluny Macpherson, in addition to David's money, which Cluny has the decency to return, David sulks during the punishing walk over the moors, making, in his own words, 'the rude, silly speech of a boy of ten'. After their quarrel Alan says to him: 'Precisely what I thought I liked about ye, was that ye never quarrelled;—and now I like ye better.' Stevenson, however, was not an easy master to imitate. Henty was.

The imperialist message which Henty and his followers proclaimed became from the 1880s onwards an orthodoxy to which parents who bought their books, and the young who read them, increasingly subscribed. This message may have failed to permeate school text–books, but it was voiced with growing vigour by writers whose works were not confined to adventure stories for boys, by poets as readily as by pamphleteers.

Kipling, in spite of the images commonly evoked by some of his verses remembered in isolation, was far from being the spokesman of the strident kind of imperialism. His was the distinction of bringing a new realism to the treatment of the activities and habits of thought of British people to whom India was not just a country of residence but a way of life. His sympathies lay with the English subaltern or the Scottish engineer serving overseas, the men who were at the outposts of empire, and not with those who stayed at home, ignoring or scorning India, deriving profits from the country perhaps, or even legislating for it. To some extent this reflected his own experiences: the contrast between, on the one hand, his happy family life in Bombay and the areas of opportunity, novelty and excitement open to a young journalist in India and, on the other, the misery he had endured as a small boy billeted on a retired naval officer in Southsea with a pitiless wife. Yet even in later years, and in spite of *Puck of Pool's Hill* and

Sussex by the Sea, Kipling with his American wife did not blend with the English countryside altogether successfully. When he wrote to Cecil Rhodes, 'England is a stuffy little place, mentally, morally and physically', it was probably more than just a momentary expression of pique.

Kipling did, it is true, have much of the equipment needed to create Newbolt Man in fiction. His attitude to women was certainly the orthodox one. His admirable biographer, Charles Carrington, recorded how as a young newspaperman Kipling was offered a bribe by an Afghan sirdar of a beautiful Kashmiri girl and a string of horses to slant an article the way the sirdar wanted. For a moment, but only for a moment, he was tempted to deviate from duty by the thought of the horses. In later life Kipling wrote to Lord Milner *à propos* of the Canadian practice of putting telephones in hotel bathrooms: 'I cannot help blushing when I am rung up by women—with nothing on but spectacles and a bath-towel.' But he was too good an observer and too serious an artist to make Newbolt Man unadorned and unanalyzed the hero of a book. He would write rather of Bobby Wicks in *Only a Subaltern* as 'the very young officer, whose devotion is given absolutely to the regiment, and whose virtues are circumscribed by the limits of his profession'. It was left to his successors as writers of fiction portraying the Indian scene, Maud Diver or Annie Steel, to make of Bobby Wicks very much more than he was or ever could be.

A more authentic voice of the new imperialism in verse was that of W. E. Henley, author of:

> In the fell clutch of circumstance
> I have not winced or cried aloud.
> Under the bludgeonings of chance
> My head is bloody, but unbowed.

These lines were in fact concerned with Henley's very private struggle when as a young man he lay for months in the Edinburgh Royal Infirmary, stricken with tuberculosis, having lost one leg and expected to lose another, lonely, poor, sustained largely by his faith in Lister, and supporting his spirit by writing poetry and teaching himself German, Italian and Spanish. But the lines were to have a less attractive echo in Henley's *The Song of the Sword,* which he dedicated to Kipling and in which he wrote of:

Sifting the nations,
The slag from the metal,
The waste and the weak
From the fit and the strong.

Of the anthology of poems which he assembled Henley wrote: 'The book is nothing if not a fighting book. It is designed to bring out such old, elementary virtues as the dignity of patriotism, the beauty of battle, the heroic quality of death.' When Queen Victoria died, Henley's memorial ode, which was published in the *Morning Post,* referred to 'dear demi-Englands, far-away isles of home, where . . . the old irresistible call, the watch-word of so many ages . . . makes men in love with toil for the race, and pain, and peril, and death'.

In his biography of Henley, John Connell, discussing Henley's editorship of the *National Observer,* wrote:

The Right had moved instinctively and pragmatically; Queen Victoria's Empire had, in fact, been built and welded without anyone knowing how it was happening. . . . Conservative Imperialism, as a political movement needing democratic, popular support, had to have voices which could be understood by the People. The *National Observer* might have supplied and trained those voices; to a limited extent it did. But what the people heard, from the mid-Nineties onward, was the *Daily Mail.*

In fact the people heard a good deal else besides from the massive publishing enterprise which launched the *Daily Mail,* an enterprise whose many successful productions included several magazines for boys.

Looking back at the age of thirty-five on what was already an exceptionally successful career, Alfred Harmsworth said in an interview: 'I knew from the first just what the people wanted to read.' His sympathetic biographers, Reginald Pound and Geoffrey Harmsworth, who in *Northcliffe* produced a more attractive portrait than has sometimes been accepted, confirmed this judgment. 'He knew what the people wanted,' they wrote, 'because their prejudices were his own.'

Harmsworth led public opinion only to the extent that he was able to sense popular trends early and clearly and to strengthen them enormously by the very success of his enterprise. His earliest editorial success came when he was put in charge of the Iliffe publication *Bicycling News* at the age of twenty-one. This was at a time when the mobility afforded by the bicycle was beginning to change the social habits of thousands, as Harmsworth clearly recognized when he made the daring innovation of appointing a woman cycling correspondent. His first publishing success, *Answers,* or, as the early title pages proclaimed, *Answers to Correspondents on Every Subject under the Sun,* specialized in producing pithy potted information, a field in which George Newnes had already succeeded spectacularly with *Tit-Bits.* Harmsworth did not invent the magazine competition, but he gave it a new popularity when *Answers* awarded £1 a week for life to the competitor who came closest to guessing the amount of gold coinage in the banking department of the Bank of England at the close of business on 4 December 1889. It was not an innovation to publish a weekly paper for women, but it was to bring it out at a penny and call it *Forget-Me-Not.* The *Sunday Companion,* by eschewing attachment to any particular denomination, soon claimed the largest circulation of any religious paper in the world, and *Comic-Cuts* ('amusing without being vulgar') may or may not have provided a generic name for a type of publication which is still abundantly with us.

With this record of success it is not surprising in retrospect to find Alfred Harmsworth and his brothers in the 1880s and early 1890s, when Henty's novels were appealing to a steadily growing public, launching several magazines for boys. *The Wonder* appeared in 1892, followed closely by *The Marvel* and *Union Jack*. This last name had also been chosen for a magazine which Henty had edited with much less success than that enjoyed by the Harmsworth family. The *Union Jack* published by the Harmsworth Amalgamated Press survived until 1933, when, significantly perhaps, it was absorbed by *Detective Weekly*. Other Harmsworth publications for boys were *Pluck Library, Boys' Home Journal, Chips, Boy's Friend* and *Triumph*. In all of them patriotism and belief in the imperial mission were unvarying features of editorial policy. Indeed in an expression of editorial satisfaction it was stated that the boys' papers of the Amalgamated Press not only encouraged physical strength, patriotism, interest in travel and exploration, and pride in the empire, but that they had in effect served as useful recruiting agencies for the armed forces.

There is no reason whatever for doubting the sincerity of Alfred Harmsworth's attachment to the Imperialist cause. His brother Cecil once said: 'Rhodes was the only statesman for whom I ever heard Alfred express unqualified admiration.' He himself told Lord Rosebery: 'The *Daily Mail* is independent and imperial,' and when the new London *Evening News* was launched it promised to afford 'an advanced democratic platform on all social matters' while 'remaining staunchly and unfalteringly Conservative in Imperial politics'. Yet, sincere though the beliefs may have been, the editorial policy of the Harmsworth boys' magazines did allow contributors to create a rather unlovable stereotype of an English boy hero and some quite deplorable stereotypes of the natives he encountered. After being reproduced through millions of words these stereotypes helped to cause a reaction of a kind neither the authors nor the publishers, presumably, intended.

'Where are you off to, Jack?' Colonel Hayden asked, as his fifteen-year-old son swung himself on to a pony held by a native syce. . . . A faint gleam of pride passed across Colonel Hayden's countenance, as he glanced at the slim, well-built figure on horseback.

In this way the scene is set in an Amalgamated Press story which is no better and no worse than hundreds of others.

Jack meets an Indian beggar, who addresses him in the second person singular, in order presumably to leave no doubt in the reader's mind that it is a native speaking. Jack's reward for a gallant effort to rescue the beggar from what appears to be imminent death from a railway train is treachery and attempted murder. But Jack is 'a quick-witted lad'. (Most boys named Jack in this kind of fiction are.) The native lures him into a cave and utters 'a shrill, mad laugh', but Jack settles the issue by bringing his water-bottle down on the head of the native, who is now called a 'yogi'. 'The latter dropped in a heap.'

A few pages later in the same Amalgamated Press annual we can read about a number of boys who take part in a cruise in the 'eastern seas'. They include 'Dick Dorrington, the leader of the Glory Hole Gang; Chip Prodgers, who could speak Hindustani like a native', and Conkey Ikestein, who is the gang's 'well-beloved and trusty treasurer'. There is a certain amount of trouble with a character named Mr Lal Tata, who complains: 'You have caused bleeding of my nasal organs.' For a time too the boys are made prisoners, or, as their chief captor puts it, 'the foreign dogs are secured, O Presence'.

'"Tis well, O Ali," said the sultan, his fat face showing a sulky grin.'

The sultan, or Sultan of Banjo, to give him his full title, is disturbed by the sound of gunfire, which causes him to leap to his feet, 'his fat, yellow face shaking like a jelly'. The dialogue which follows includes such statements as: '"That pudding-faced rooster is the sultan. Collar him low!"' Conkey Ikestein wants to loot the palace, but Dick Dorrington stands firm, and at the end we learn: 'You can now send a cable to any part of the world from Great Banjo Island.'

In short, provided the boys are British and brave and conform to certain standards of what is called 'honourable' conduct—you don't loot palaces unless your name is Conkey Ikestein—the field of permissible behaviour is a pretty wide one. But it is all rather far removed from the patriotism of Newbolt, which made such a favourable impression on Yeats, 'the patriotism that lays burdens upon a man, and not the patriotism that takes burdens off'.

The change was of course a consequence of putting the ideal of patriotism, indeed the standards of Newbolt Man, through the mangle of vulgarization which the Harmsworth publications provided.

These publications did not reach the nadir of radical, jingoist journalism. Horatio Bottomley was to touch even lower depths. But of the many and complex causes of the prolonged reaction against British imperialism, both at home and overseas, one which is far from negligible is to be found in the characters, exploits and, perhaps most important, phraseology of the numerous Dick Dorringtons and the numerous Glory Hole gangs spawned by the Amalgamated Press from the 1880s through to the 1930s.

CHAPTER FIVE

Newbolt Man and the
Historical Novel of Adventure

In the 1880s and 1890s the historical novel of adventure flourished at a number of literary levels. While Henty was steadily turning out books which presented young Newbolt Man with minimal variations of character but in a rich variety of settings, some enviable reputations were being made by authors who wrote for adult as much as for juvenile readers and who also plundered the history books to find stories of adventure. Probably at no period before, and at no period since, was there so much concern in English popular fiction with the recreation of the past, particularly those past glories of England which were attributable to her men of action.

This vogue was in part a response to the stirrings of patriotism and of a sense of imperial mission which Henley sensed and recorded and of which there was indeed abundant evidence. But there were also powerful literary influences. One of these was the extraordinary popularity of the works of Alexandre Dumas *père,* which not only commanded a huge readership but gave rise to something of a literary cult, Thackeray and Stevenson being among the self-proclaimed Dumas addicts. (Of novelists whose works have been translated from French, only Georges Simenon and, arguably, Jules Verne seem to have enjoyed a comparable cult–cum–popularity success in England.) Another important literary influence was that of Andrew Lang, anthropologist and translator of Homer, author of fairy–tales and leader writer for the *Daily News.*

Lang had an exceptional talent for most forms of *belles-lettres,* the kind of talent which used to find ready outlets in the essay and light verse. He also had a wide-ranging interest in literature of many kinds, abundant energy and powers of application. All this and a certain amount of luck served to raise him to that eminence seldom reached by more than one or two critics in a generation, from which he had the power to make an author's reputation overnight by a eulogistic review. It was a power he used more than once when reviewing novels of adventure by hitherto little-known authors.

An appreciable proportion of Lang's own large literary output consisted of historical romances, and he even tried collaborating with both A.E.W. Mason and Henry Rider Haggard. His success as a romantic novelist was limited, but his delight in the genre continued undiminished. In his boyhood his favourite literary hero had been Amyas Leigh; he admired Newbolt's *Admirals All,* and he was keenly interested in cricket. These tastes and interests not only influenced his literary judgments, but produced a dichotomy in which his literary standing was sharply divided from his attitude towards literary creation. Richard Le Galliene summed this up well with the comment: 'Mr Lang, perhaps the most literary temperament that ever lived, would have you believe that to write a good book is nothing compared with playing a good game of golf.' Henry James, more scathingly, wrote to Stevenson of Lang using 'his beautiful thin facility to write everything down to the lowest level of Philistine twaddle'. Henley even less charitably described Lang as 'a shystering little piffler', but Henley's comments on other literary figures tended to be governed by the degree of physical pain he was himself suffering when he made them.

Lang defended himself against the charge that he overrated

certain contemporary books by stating that 'late Victorian novels are not the great things of human literature, and a reader may blamelessly amuse or depress himself with them as he will'. But he gave a more revealing explanation of why his literary sympathies lay where they did when he drew an analogy between exploring, in a novel, the secret of a girl's heart and exploring her bedroom. On one occasion he even wrote: 'I cannot go so far as to despise the novel of character, but I do "bar" the novel of bad characters.' Not surprisingly writers with an inclination to present their heroes in the uncomplicated form of Newbolt Man found in Lang a ready champion.

One writer whom Lang helped to advance, and who also owed an evident debt to Dumas, was Stanley Weyman. Weyman was one of those novelists who, after showing little compulsive urge to write in their early days, are induced by external circumstances to have a try at authorship, and promptly achieve a huge success. The incentive in his case was the virtual absence of either work or money arising from his bar practice, and the form and subjects of his early novels were derived largely from his reading of Dumas and his study of French history. With the publication of *The Man in Black* and *Under the Red Robe* he was even hoisted by injudicious critics on to a level comparable with that of Stevenson.

Having established his name by excursions into French history, Weyman later took to portraying English heroes set in an English past, *The Castle Inn,* published in 1898, being one of his best-known novels in this vein. *The Castle Inn* is a romance of the road, a genre of novel much favoured by English writers of fiction, by those of the calibre of Sterne as readily as by those of the calibre of Jeffrey Farnol. The period in which *The Castle Inn* is set is the mid–eighteenth century, and the hero, Sir George Soane, early on in the book encounters a beautiful girl on the road from London to Oxford. She is known as Julia Masterson and is the adopted daughter of the porter of Pembroke College. Lord Dunborough, a young man with a violent temper and vicious habits, has designs on Julia, but in a drunken brawl he and some of his friends cause the death of Masterson.

After Soane and Dunborough have fought a duel, in which Dunborough is wounded, the scene shifts to the Castle Inn in Marlborough, where all the principal *dramatis personae* assemble. These include Soane himself; Julia, now dressed as a lady and attended by her mother and a lawyer named Fishwick; Dunborough; Dunborough's formidable mother, attended by a cowardly and rascally Oxford tutor in holy orders; the great Earl of Chatham, suffering from gout, and his attendant physician, Dr Addington.

Soane is expecting to inherit a fortune, which alone can save him from his debts, but he learns from Addington that there is another claimant to the estate, an unknown cousin. When we learn that money was mysteriously provided to pay for Julia's education we sense that she must be the claimant and cousin. The lawyer Fishwick has in fact come to the inn in the hope of being received by Chatham and advancing her claim.

Dunborough arranges to have Julia kidnapped, and Soane and the lawyer set off in search of her. She has a series of adventures and narrow escapes from various aristocratic rakes, and the chase takes Soane and Fishwick to Bristol. Here Fishwick accidentally finds an entry in a burial book, which proves that Soane's girl cousin died in infancy. Julia is in fact the orphaned daugther of a teacher of French and has no claims on the fortune Soane is expecting.

Julia's reaction is to take a job as a domestic servant, but Soane duly rescues her from this and marries her. Chatham, impressed by Fishwick's honesty in destroying his own client's case, appoints him to the office of Clerk of the Leases in the Forest of Dean.

In his portrayal of his hero, no less than in his descriptions of inn and coaching scenes and the references to historical events, Weyman tried conscientiously to be faithful to the period of which he was writing. Soane is said to live in an age in which an adventure of gallantry was the only adventure in vogue. He belongs to 'the inner circle of fashion, to which neither rank nor wealth, nor parts, nor power, of necessity admitted'. He has been an irresponsible gambler, and when he sets out in pursuit of Julia the author asks: 'What of Sir George, hurled suddenly out of his age and world—the age *des philosophes* and the smooth world of White's?' The answer, for all Weyman's concern with period, is that Sir George adapts himself as readily to the challenge as any late–nineteenth–century specimen of Newbolt Man would have done. This is not altogether surprising in view of some of the characteristics his author gives him.

'His face lost the air of affected refinement—which was then the mode, and went perfectly with a wig and ruffles—and appeared in its true cast, plain and strong, yet not uncomely.' He also has 'a pair of grey eyes, keen, humorous and kindly'. When Addington describes him as a fine gentleman from White's 'a different look came into his face'. During the chase he shows 'a grim coolness', and Fishwick is so impressed by his power of command in action that his 'smaller personality' goes out in admiration to Soane's 'splendid personality'. For all the sophistication of his background Julia finds him 'little versed in woman's ways'..

Chippinge, which was published eight years after *The Castle Inn,* was another of Weyman's romances of the road. The hero, Arthur Vaughan, meets another beautiful girl, in his case on the Bath road. She goes by the name of Mary Smith and is a schoolteacher. Money has been mysteriously provided for her education too. The period is the early 1830s, and Vaughan, who has expectations from his cousin, Sir Robert Vermuyden, quarrels with Sir Robert because of their different attitudes towards the Reform Bill. Believing as he does in the principle of reform, Vaughan refuses what is in effect a bribe of £80,000 to allow Sir Robert to continue to control Chippinge as a pocket borough, stands for Parliament himself, and is returned. After a promising start to his political career he becomes disillusioned by the cynical attitude to matters of principle taken by Whigs as readily as by Tories.

The climax of the story takes place in Bristol during the Reform riots. Before taking up politics Vaughan resigned his Army commission, having 'sickened of the idle life of an officer in peace time'. In the face of riots his status as a maintainer of law and order is therefore a wholly amateur one, but this does not prevent him from becoming the saviour of Bristol. The officer commanding troops is too fearful of causing bloodshed. Another officer, Bob Flixton, who has designs on Mary Smith, is an unreasoning hothead. So it is Vaughan, placed in charge of the constables, who succeeds, through his coolness, courage and calculated disobedience of orders, in saving Bristol from the 'low Irish' and 'the rabble who thirsted for the strong ale in the cellars'. Sir Robert Vermuyden is also in Bristol during the riots, having come to visit Mary Smith, who is discovered to be his long–lost daughter. He too behaves with great fortitude, Vaughan and he are reconciled, and the problem of who inherits what is again satisfactorily solved.

In *Chippinge,* which has been rated as among the best of Weyman's novels, the period fixtures and fittings are presented with scrupulous care, but Weyman barely troubles to saddle Arthur Vaughan with the kind of period characteristics he conferred on Sir George Soane. 'It is doubtful,' he writes of Vaughan, 'if he had ever seen the inside of Almack's. But his features were strong and intellectual, and the keen grey eyes which looked so boldly on the world could express both humour and good–humour.' After his early encounter with Mary Smith he fears she may think him 'a libertine, who aimed at putting himself on a footing of intimacy with her', but reassurance is given in the statement that 'Vaughan was no Lothario'. Vaughan is enough of an idealist to think of the Reform Bill as one 'which must create a new England, and for many a new world'. This belief is not destroyed, but his triumph in Bristol gives him a new perspective. '"After all, that is what I am good for," he told himself as he stood to take breath after a *mêlée* which was at once the most serious and the last. . . . "Better a good blow than a bad speech!"'

As a young man Arthur Conan Doyle was also attracted to the historical novel of adventure. Describing his plans for *Micah Clarke,* which is set in the seventeenth century, he wrote:

I chose a historical novel . . . because it seemed to me the one way of combining a certain amount of literary dignity with those scenes of action and adventure which were natural to my young and ardent mind. I had always felt great sympathy for the Puritans, who, after all, whatever their peculiarities, did represent political liberty and earnestness in religion.

In *The White Company* he projected Englishmen of the kind he admired into an even earlier period of history, that of the fourteenth century, prefacing the book with the dedication: 'To the hope of the future, the reunion of the English–speaking races, this little chronicle of our common ancestry is dedicated.' The little chronicle is largely a record of various forms of physical combat permeated, and relieved, by the spirit of chivalry or fair play.

The action of *The White Company* opens in Beaulieu Abbey, which two young men are compelled to leave. One known as Big John has been dismissed for such sins as drinking more than his fair share of beer and holding a brother face down in the piscatorium. The other, Alleyne Edricson, has been educated in the abbey, but at the age of twenty is obliged by the terms of his father's will to spend a year in the outside world before deciding whether to adopt the monastic life. Soon after leaving the abbey John and Alleyne fall in with a soldier named Samkin Aylward, who describes himself as 'a true English bowman'. Big John is easily persuaded by the bowman to seek a life of adventure over-seas, but Alleyne is determined to visit his brother, the Socman of Minstead. His encounter with his brother is a brief one, for he finds him on the point of exercising force against a beautiful girl. The brothers fight, and Alleyne succeeds in saving the girl. He then goes in search of his companions of the road and finds them at Twynham Castle as members of a body of freebooters known as the White Company under the command of Sir Nigel Loring. The beautiful girl Alleyne has saved proves to be Sir Nigel's daughter, and Sir Nigel chooses Alleyne as his squire. The White Company then sets off for France, for 'the old game was afoot once more'. The old game includes a sea battle with pirates, various individual battles, most of them fought over points of honour, and a great jousting contest, which is in effect a five-a-side match between England and the Rest of the World. With the score at two–all Sir Nigel decides the contest by a victory over a burly German.

Although precluded at first from taking part in the knightly contests, Alleyne distinguishes himself by his courage and coolness, and after a particularly daring exploit he is knighted by the Black Prince. This emboldens him to confess to Sir Nigel his love for his daughter, and he returns to England only just in time to win her, for the daughter, having been informed that there were no survivors from the White Company, was on the point of entering a nunnery.

There are in effect two heroes, Sir Nigel and Alleyne. Sir Nigel is quite uncomplicated. He is a small man with a gentle manner and given to understatement, but immediately after his appearance in the book we learn something of his quality when a huge black bear breaks loose in Twynham Castle. Everyone else is terrified, but Sir Nigel brings the bear to heel by flicking it across the snout with a handkerchief and saying 'saucy! saucy!' From then on no further doubt can be entertained about his power of command, and it is a power which he exercises with unfailing courtesy. He finds writing a letter to his wife rather beyond his powers and needs Alleyne's help. 'Twenty years of camp life', we learn too, 'had left him more at ease in the lists than in a lady's boudoir.'

Alleyne, on the other hand, develops from a cloistered background, having 'a nature which had unfolded far from the boisterous joys and sorrows of the world'. He is skilled in music and painting, though after the early pages we hear nothing of these accomplishments, and we can guess the kind of man he will become when we learn of 'a set of the mouth and a prominence of the chin which relieved him of any trace of effeminacy'. Although his family no longer owns much of the land it once held, Alleyne's father could trace his 'pure Saxon lineage' back three hundred years, and when Alleyne has his first physical combat, that with his brother, there was a ring in his voice and a flash in his eyes which promised that the blow would follow quick at the heels of the word. For a moment the blood of the long line of hot-headed thanes was too strong for the soft whisperings of the doctrine of meekness and mercy. He was conscious of a fierce wild thrill through his nerves and a throb of mad gladness at his heart, as his real human self burst for an instant the bonds of custom and of teaching which had held it so long.

After that there is no stopping his advance in the world of the White Company. In swordsmanship and courage he is the equal of any outside the knightly ranks, and in other respects he is superior to most. One example of this superiority comes early in the book, when he protests against the singing of a bawdy song in an inn. Whereas Samkin Aylward is presented as a lusty woman-izer, Alleyne's future wife finds him awkward and ill at ease in her presence.

Unfortunately—for Sherlock Holmes addicts at least—Conan Doyle's preoccupation with the historical novel of adventure was not confined to his youth. The character of Nigel Loring interested and attracted him so much that fifteen years after the publication of *The White Company* the novel entitled *Sir Nigel* appeared. The action in *Sir Nigel* takes place in an earlier phase of the Hundred Years' War than that depicted in *The White Company* and consists largely of the exploits of the young Nigel Loring, 'with his lion heart and with the blood of a hundred soldiers thrilling in his veins', to whom 'a lie was an impossibility'. Nigel's first physical triumph is the breaking-in of a fierce, proud horse which has been terrifying some Cistercian monks. This conquest is in effect the counterpart to the victory over the school bully which was an essential ingredient of other popular works of fiction. Nigel then proceeds to deal with a lascivious hunchback, whose house is 'a den of profligacy and vice', and who is on the point of seducing Nigel's future sister-in-law. (Alleyne Edricson is not called upon to cope with any hunchbacks, but he and Big John do mete out summary justice to a negro who is trying to rob an old woman. Conan Doyle concedes that the number of negroes to be found in the English countryside in the fourteenth century was limited.) The subsequent encounters in *Sir Nigel* include those sea and land battles which readers must have come to expect, and there is also a thirty–a–side Anglo–Breton jousting contest. This the Bretons rather surprisingly win, but their victory is attributed to a 'foul trick'.

Of Nigel himself we learn that 'as far as physical feats went, to vault barebacked upon a horse, to hit a running hare with a crossbow–bolt, or to climb the angle of a castle courtyard, were feats which had come by nature to the young Squire; but it was very different with music, which had called for many a weary hour of irksome work'. His future sister–in–law, finding him much less susceptible to her advances than the hunchback, says to him: 'Oh cold of speech! Surely you were bred for the cloisters and not a lady's bower, Nigel.'

The Loring family, for all their past greatness and the services they have rendered to English kings, are now impoverished, the main cause of their troubles being the avarice and trickery of the Cistercian monks. The author in this work no longer confines himself to scorning the 'soft whisperings of the doctrine of meekness and mercy'. He presents us uncompromisingly with a priest who held the brazier while a French robber baron put out the eyes of an English prisoner. Newbolt Man has emerged unmistakeably, though in fourteenth–century costume, but the doctrine of muscular Christianity, it may be thought, has reached the point at which the Christianity is quietly dropped.

In his frequent travels through Europe Stanley Weyman was sometimes accompanied by Hugh Stowell Scott, who wrote under the name of H. Seton Merriman, largely in order to avoid the displeasure of a family who had procured him a post in the office of a Lloyd's underwriter. Scott's death at the age of forty–one was a loss to the kind of fiction which is more than merely entertainment. As a writer of historical novels he is, in my judgment, much more easily readable than either Weyman or Doyle.

Among the best of his novels was *Barlasch of the Guard,* in which the atmosphere of Danzig and its surrounding territory during the Napoleonic wars is evoked with considerable skill. Two cousins, Louis and Charles d'Arragon, find themselves on different sides in the conflict, Charles being a secret Napoleonic agent and Louis having served in the British Navy. Charles marries Désirée, the daughter of a French aristocrat who has settled in Danzig under the name of Antoine Sebastian and who is earning his living as a dancing master. Charles is killed during the retreat from Moscow, and Louis in his efforts to find him undergoes a variety of dangers. He finds Charles's dead body and returns to Danzig to claim Désirée as his wife.

The central figure and, to some extent, the hero of the book is a cunning old soldier of the Napoleonic guard named Barlasch, who has a talent for finding a comfortable billet until he finally gives his life for Désirée. Louis d'Arragon, the other hero, who has an English mother, is a more conventional figure, 'open and simple and practical, like the life he led'. Antoine Sebastian says to him:

'I am honoured to make the acquaintance of Monsieur le Marquis.'

'Oh, you must not call me that,' replied d'Arragon with a short laugh. 'I am an English sailor—that is all.'

Louis d'Arragon's face is 'usually quiet and still; a combination of that contemplative calm which characterizes seafaring faces, and the clean–cut immobility of a racial type developed by hereditary duties of self–control and command'. A Pole named Colonel de Casimir considers himself a match for both d'Arragon and Désirée in quickness of perception, rapidity of thought and glibness of speech, but 'there was a steadiness in d'Arragon's eyes which rarely goes with dullness of wit'. Barlasch feels much the same. 'He's a strong one, that,' he says as he holds up his hand to indicate that it would be unwise to trifle with Louis d'Arragon.

In *The Three Gentleman* A.E.W. Mason, an even more gifted writer than Merriman, created a character who appears in three different incarnations. The first is as Attilius Scaurus, a young Roman who because of his extravagance is banished by his family to Britain, where he distinguishes himself as a soldier. The second is as Anthony Scan, who serves Sir Francis Walsingham as a spy and plays a major part in the defeat of the Spanish armada. The third is as Adrian Shard, private secretary to a modern British politician. The code to which all three subscribe is discussed by Adrian Shard's father, who after a lifetime of soldiering in India has retired to Jamaica because of his asthma. Father and son listen in Jamaica to a radio transmission of Big Ben chiming midnight, and the father then speaks of 'a race of young men who'll serve, not for rewards, not for the game, not for a fine big name in the newspapers, not even for real fame, though that's an end worthy enough, but just for service' sake—service to the King's realm'. The concept of service to an empire is the one constant in an otherwise changing scene, and it is clearly implied that the old Roman empire is the only acceptable historical counterpart to the modern British one. There is even a certain geographical continuity in the imperial concept. "'If ever you're an Emperor,'" Attilius Scaurus's commanding officer says to him, "'take an old soldier's advice and watch night and day, winter and summer, your North-West frontier. It was the danger in Latium. It is the danger in Britain. The Gods in their wisdom . . . have ordained a riddle worthy of old Oedipus which all Empires must solve or fall—the riddle of the North-West frontier.'"

The qualities which Sir George Soane and Arthur Vaughan, Sir Nigel Loring and Louis d'Arragon have in common can be found in the heroes of plenty of other writers who delved into the history books for their material. They can be found, for example, in the characters of Jeffrey Farnol by readers who are willing to penetrate through the thickets of a language which continually sprouts such words as 'mayhap' and 'maugre'. (Farnol even used the phrase 'maugre my reader's weariness' and got away with it.) But perhaps the best known, and for a long time the best loved, of all English heroes of historical novels created in the twentieth century is an interesting blend of Newbolt Man and another kind of traditional hero of popular fiction. This character made his first appearance in a novel which was rejected by more than a dozen publishers. Indeed if the author had not produced, in collaboration with her husband, a dramatized version which provided acceptable parts for Fred Terry and Julia Neilson, it might conceivably never have achieved the dignity of print. The novel was Baroness Orczy's *The Scarlet Pimpernel*.

There are plenty of 'mayhaps' in the Baroness's works too. Lady Blakeney wonders whether 'mayhap she was looking into those dear, lazy, laughing eyes for the last time', just as Chauvelin wonders whether 'mayhap his enemy was lying in wait for him down below'. The dialogue is enlivened by such expressions as 'name of a name of a dog' and 'pardi', which it may be permissible to assume is the U equivalent of 'pardon'. Swarms of adjectives too buzz round the reader's head like bluebottles.

> Her grey hair, lank and unruly, was partially hidden by an ample floating veil of an indefinite shade of grey, and from her meagre shoulders and arms, her garment—it was barely a gown—descended in straight, heavy, shapeless folds. In front of her was a small table, on it a large crystal globe, which rested on a stand of black wood, exquisitely carved and inlaid with mother-of-pearl, and beside it a small metal box.

But the personality of Sir Percy Blakeney triumphs over all this as readily as it does over the henchmen of Robespierre.

In the first novel the identity of the Scarlet Pimpernel is not overtly revealed until towards the end, and Blakeney has therefore to be disguised to some extent as a kind of silly-ass, indolent nobleman. The disguise is a thin one.

Tall, above the average, even for an Englishman, broad-shouldered, massively built, he would have been called unusually good-looking but for a certain lazy expression in his deep-set blue eyes, and that perpetual inane laugh which seemed to disfigure his strong, clearly-cut mouth.

The characters of the Scarlet Pimpernel's devoted followers, on the other hand, can be revealed without any restrictions. Lord Anthony Dewhurst is 'a very perfect type of a young English gentleman—tall, well set up, broad of shoulders and merry of face'. He is also 'a good sportsman, a lively companion, a courteous well-bred man of the world, with not too much brains to spoil his temper'. The face of Sir Andrew Ffoulkes shines with enthusiasm, hero-worship, love and admiration when he speaks of the Scarlet Pimpernel, and when the Comtesse de Tournay de Basserive asks him why he and his friends spend their money and risk their lives to save French aristocrats from the guillotine, Sir Andrew replies: 'We are a nation of sportsmen, you know.'

In the later books Blakeney, now identified as the Scarlet Pimpernel, can dispense with the veneer of stupidity and becomes the masterful leader with an astounding talent for disguises. Theresia Cabarrus, who is herself 'a bundle of feminine caprice', pictures 'the tall, magnificent figure; the lazy, laughing eyes; the slender hand that looked so firm and strong amidst the billows of exquisite lace'. Blakeney is also of course as chivalrous as he is courageous, and even his enemy Chauvelin, in a moment of anxiety for his own safety, comforts himself by saying: '"Bah! Assassination, and in the dark, are not the Englishman's ways."'

Sir Percy Blakeney differs from Newbolt Man in a number of respects, the differences being probably all attributable to the nature of his creator. Unlike the upper-middle-class stereotype, whose creator might confer a title on him but who remained upper middle class, Blakeney is an aristocrat, a kind of being for whom many women writers of popular fiction have had a weakness. Dorothy Sayers was later to choose as her detective Lord Peter Wimsey, and even the New Zealander Ngaio Marsh, having selected a police inspector named Alleyne to solve her crimes, equipped him in time with a wealth of aristocratic family connections. Blakeney did at least have good manners, which is more than can be said of Wimsey.

Blakeney is 'blindly, passionately in love' with his wife, who, far from being a Daisy or a Violet, is a former actress at the Comédie Francaise and the cleverest woman in Europe, 'with all a woman's most fascinating foibles, all a woman's most lovable sins'. A relationship of this kind does not come within the range of the conventionally sexless hero, but for obvious reasons women writers did not create Newbolt Man in his sexless form. Sexless schoolboys, yes, but not sexless male adults.

Nevertheless, as a sportsman, a leader of devoted followers, all enjoying amateur status, as one who handles a schooner 'as well as any master mariner', is modest, given to understatement and jests lightly in the presence of danger, Blakeney is not unrelated to Newbolt Man. It might even be said that he was as close an approximation as could be created by a woman writer who was not herself English. The Baroness Orczy married an Englishman, but she did not herself come to live in England until she was fifteen, and it may well be that her picture of aristocratic Englishmen of the past was to an appreciable extent formed during her childhood in Hungary and France.

The writers whom Andrew Lang championed, Weyman, Mason and the others, gave Newbolt Man plenty of scope for adventure in historical novels, but in general it was not in this genre of fiction that he found the most fruitful and natural setting for his activities. Perhaps the idiom was an impediment. Terms such as 'methinks' and 'quotha', to which Doyle among others was addicted, were not easily compatible with the utterances of Newbolt Man in his purest form.

From the 1880s onwards Newbolt Man tended to reach his fullest stature in one or other of two different but related literary genres. In both of these the setting was contemporary: in one the action took place overseas, in the other at home. Both genres were to provide him with some of his finest hours in novels commanding huge sales and a public which was continually eager for more. Of the writers of these novels some of the ablest were men who were strongly influenced by South Africa, in particular by the South African war, a war which, significantly, also gave rise to the Boy Scout movement.

CHAPTER SIX

White Man's Burden

Henry Rider Haggard sailed for South Africa at the age of nineteen as a member of the staff of the newly appointed Lieutenant-Governor of Natal, Sir Henry Bulwer. He arrived in Cape Colony in August 1875. The next year he was sent on a mission deep into Basuto territory, where white men had rarely been seen, and at the age of twenty-one, without any legal training, he was appointed master and registrar of the Pretoria high court. After the disaster to the British forces at Isandhlwana at the hands of the Zulus he took a leading part in forming the Pretoria Horse and became its adjutant.

As a young man Edgar Wallace enlisted as a soldier in the Royal West Kent Regiment and was posted to South Africa. During the Boer war he served as a medical orderly and later as correspondent, first for Reuter's and then for the *Daily Mail*. After the war he became editor of the *Rand Daily Mail,* an appointment he held for about nine months.

Arthur Conan Doyle at the age of forty volunteered for military service in South Africa on Christmas Eve, 1899. In a letter to his mother explaining his reasons, he wrote: 'I have perhaps the strongest influence over young men, especially young athletic sporting men, of any one in England (bar Kipling). That being so, it is really important that I should give them a lead.' Soon after his arrival in the war zone he was appointed senior physician to a field hospital.

John Buchan, after becoming assistant private secretary to Lord Milner, served for two years in South Africa, travelling extensively in the territory of the union and playing a role of some political importance in the post-war settlement.

The total readership of the tales of mystery or adventure produced by these four men—Rider Haggard, Edgar Wallace, Conan Doyle and John Buchan—defies calculation.

Doyle and Buchan were both strongly influenced in their political beliefs and their philosophy by their experiences in South Africa. On returning to England Doyle wrote a work of history entitled *The Great Boer War,* became an outspoken supporter of Joseph Chamberlain, and stood for Parliament as a Liberal Unionist candidate, though without success. Buchan too wrote books about South Africa, *The African Colony* and *A Lodge in the Wilderness,* and with him the experience went even deeper. It did much to form his belief in an association of free nations, transcending nationalism and advancing far beyond the concept of trusteeship, which was to be a guiding principle in a career culminating in his appointment as Governor–General of Canada. Other writers too commanding huge readerships were deeply influenced by the South African war. It was in South Africa that Kipling first saw troops under fire. On returning to England he had a drill hall built in Rottingdean, formed a volunteer company and a branch of the Navy League, and became chairman of their managing committees.

As writers of popular fiction Doyle and Buchan both provided overseas settings for a number of their tales, but the most famous of their characters were wholly or largely London–based. Sherlock Holmes is inseparable in the mind from Baker Street, and we first meet Buchan's Richard Hannay in London after he has made his 'pile'. Hannay and his associates undertake adventures in a number of continents, but they radiate out from, and periodically return to, what Richard Usborne in his witty and perceptive study of Buchan and other writers called 'clubland'. Haggard and Wallace, by contrast, achieved their first notable successes as writers of fiction by drawing on their experiences of the African continent and giving their stories African settings.

After he came back to England Haggard published a book entitled *Cetywayo and His White Neighbours*. 154 copies were sold. He also published two fairly conventional novels, whose reception made him decide to abandon all attempts to write fiction and to concentrate on a legal career. Then, after discussing Stevenson's *Treasure Island* with one of his brothers, he decided to try to write an adventure story. The outcome was *King Solomon's Mines,* written in six weeks and published in 1885, and as fine an example as any of the kind of fiction known in the 1880s as a 'romance'. It was fully in keeping with the characteristics of a romance of the period that Allan Quatermain, the narrator of *King Solomon's Mines,* should give an early assurance that 'there is not a petticoat in the whole history'. Some five years after completing *King Solomon's Mines* Haggard wrote: 'Really good romance writing is perhaps the most difficult art practised by the sons of man.' This statement appeared in an article in the *Contemporary Review,* in which he described French naturalism in fiction as 'that accursed thing' and added: 'Whatever there is that is carnal and filthy, is here brought into prominence, and thrust before the reader's eyes.'

King Solomon's Mines is dedicated to 'all the big boys and little boys who read it'. A number of Haggard's other dedications are also illuminating. He dedicated *Allan Quatermain* to his son, expressing the hope that he might reach the highest rank attainable, 'the state and dignity of an English gentleman'. Sadly, the boy died too young for the hope to be fulfilled. *The Way of the Spirit* is dedicated to Kipling with the words: 'Both of us believe that there are higher things in life than the weaving of stories well or ill, and according to our separate occasions strive to fulfil this faith.'

Allan Quatermain apologizes at the outset in *King Solomon's Mines* for his 'blunt way of writing', explaining that he is more used to handling a rifle than a pen. Though 'born a gentleman', he was earning his living in the 'old Colony' and Natal at an age when other boys were at school, and his reading is confined to the Bible and the *Ingoldsby Legends*. But Quatermain, the grizzled trader, hunter and explorer, who periodically and most unconvincingly refers to his own timidity and fears, is not the principal hero of the book. This is Sir Henry Curtis, who has 'a thick yellow beard, clear-cut features and large grey eyes set deep in his head'. Quatermain likens him to an ancient Viking and declares he has never seen a better looking man. Curtis proves to be the best fighting man in the book, but he is also a scholar, 'having taken a high degree in classics'.

Curtis has a companion who joins him in an expedition which begins with a search for Curtis's lost brother and leads to the discovery of the mines. This is Captain John Good, R.N. Of him Quatermain writes:

> I asked a page or two back, what is a gentleman? I'll answer that question now: a Royal Naval officer is, in a general sort of way, though of course there may be a black sheep among them here and there. I fancy it's just the wide seas and the breath of God's winds that wash their hearts and blow the bitterness out of their minds and make them what they ought to be.

Good appears to have only one shortcoming:

> 'Curse it!' said Good—for I am sorry to say he had a habit of using strong language when excited—contracted, no doubt, in the course of his nautical career.

Finally there is Umbopa, who is well over six feet tall, broad and shapely. His dignity matches his appearance, and Quatermain even finds himself comparing Umbopa with Curtis. Umbopa is eventually discovered to be Ignosi, the deposed but rightful king of the Kukuanas. Having gained his knowledge of fighting in Africa when Zulus, not Boers, were the enemy, Haggard's sympathies were firmly established. The Boer, he once wrote, 'has no romance in him, nor any of the higher feelings and aspirations that are found in almost every other race. . . . Unlike the Zulu he despises, there is little of the gentleman in his composition.' Later writers of fiction who gained their knowledge from the Boer war tended, by contrast, to present Boer characters rather sympathetically. One such was Buchan's Peter Pienaar. This was in keeping with a tendency, widespread in Britain in the first decade of the present century, to regard the Boers much as supporters of the champion county might regard a lowly placed county cricket team which in a crucial match, although beaten in the end, had not only led the champions on the first innings, but had done so by virtue of such estimable qualities as team spirit and smartness in the field.

The four heroes of *King Solomon's Mines* represent four different types whom Haggard admired: the white explorer, the aristocratic leader, the conventional English gentleman and the warrior native king. As the sole hero of a book a good representative example of one who remains true to Haggard's ideals in the face of continual danger is Robert Seymour in *Benita*.

Seymour is described on the first page as 'a tall man about thirty years of age'. On the next page, when there is talk of a ship's dance, he announces that his dancing days are over. Later a more detailed description is given. 'His face was clean cut, not particularly handsome, since, their fineness notwithstanding, his features lacked regularity.' These features are, however, 'redeemed to some extent by the steady and cheerful grey eyes', and 'for the rest, he was broad-shouldered and well set-up, sealed with the indescribable stamp of the English gentleman'.

Seymour is excessively modest when he first talks about himself to Benita, the heroine. He claims to be 'one of the most useless persons in the world, an undistinguished member of what is called in England the "leisured class". He can do little, he says, worth doing except shoot straight, and he describes himself as ruined and almost hopeless at the age of thirty-two. In fact he still has about £2,000. (The date of the book's publication was 1906.)

When the ship in which he and Benita are travelling goes down off the coast of Africa, Seymour behaves with exemplary calm, courage and self-sacrifice. He gives his place in one of the ship's lifeboats to a woman with a child and tries to swim for the shore. So far, so good. It is in the later adventures in Africa that some of the human relationships become a little disturbing.

Benita's father, though he is one of the Lincolnshire Cliffords and was educated at Eton and Oxford, has gone through a prolonged period of drunkenness during which he came very much under the influence of his trading partner, a Jew named Jacob Meyer. Clifford becomes a reformed alcoholic, but Meyer's shortcomings, being racial, are not so easily put right. Meyer is the dominant partner throughout, yet we read of the doings of 'Mr Clifford and Meyer'.

Some of the later adventures are not unlike those in *King Solomon's Mines,* and the four principal characters, Benita, Seymour, Clifford and Meyer, are besieged and in grave danger. Meyer in fact behaves with great courage, at one point saving the lives of Benita and Seymour by picking off a few hostile Matabele with his rifle, yet shortly afterwards we read of 'the gentle, foreign voice of Meyer speaking his sarcastic words of greeting'.

Meyer's principal offence is that he desires Benita, though, cooped up as they all are at close quarters and living at a high degree of tension, he shows remarkable restraint, especially as he has the advantage of mesmeric powers. Eventually he weakens, and after putting Benita under a spell he kisses her. This is decisive.

> She was no longer afraid of Jacob Meyer; that coward kiss of his had struck off the shackles which bound her to him. Her mind had been subject to his mind, but now that his physical nature was brought into play, his mental part had lost its hold upon her.

On hearing what has happened Clifford exclaims: 'The dirty Jew! The villain!' Seymour, by contrast, icily warns Meyer at the end to 'keep Miss Clifford's name off your lips, or I will hand you over to those Kaffirs to be dealt with as you deserve'. By this time Seymour has also kissed Benita. 'He drew her to him and kissed her passionately for the first time; then, as though ashamed of himself, let her go.'

That Rider Haggard should have created the heroes he did is in no way surprising in the light of what is known about his background, his tastes and his character. He had the compelling urge to be accorded amateur status which was characteristic of so many successful English writers of adventure stories until quite recently. On establishing himself in Ditchingham House in Norfolk in 1889 he led the life which his position demanded, taking a keen, indeed scientific interest in farming, serving as a magistrate, contesting a parliamentary seat, albeit unsuccessfully, and reading in a resonant voice from the old family Bible to his entire household assembled in the hall for family prayers. There is plenty of evidence indeed that he chose to regard himself as a country gentleman rather than as a writer, although he was fully aware that it was on his writing that his livelihood depended.

Haggard was generally ill at ease with women and seems to have found it difficult to communicate with them. He had a strong aversion to what were known in his time as 'smoking-room yarns', and when he was accused of advocating infidelity in one of his books he was so shocked that he tried to have the book withdrawn. Politically, he and Kipling tended to move together, and after the war of 1914-18 they were instrumental in forming the Liberty League to combat the advance of Bolshevism. In his well-documented biography of Haggard Morton Cohen equates him closely with the older of his two familiar types of hero.

the narrator, an ageing, experienced, wise gentleman, who is more complex than his younger companion. . . . He is not a universal man. He is far better with a machete in the African bush than with a tea-cup in the English drawing-room; he has learned more from nature than from books.

In his way of life, tastes and habits, both before and after he had achieved success, Edgar Wallace differed so widely from Rider Haggard that the two men might be thought to have had virtually nothing in common other than exceptional popularity as writers and that first-hand knowledge of Africa which set them both on the road to fame. Wallace was the illegitimate son of an unsuccessful actress and was brought up as an orphan in the family of a Billingsgate fish-porter. He left school at twelve, had various jobs, such as selling newspapers and delivering milk, which he was unable to hold down, and clearly improved such commercial prospects as he had when he enlisted in the Army. When the opportunity presented itself he wrote to make money. He aspired to be a professional, and he became one. Kipling, whom he met in South Africa, told him after he had had some verses published in the *Cape Times:* 'For God's sake don't take to literature as a profession. Literature is a splendid mistress, but a bad wife.' This did not deter him, and he is on record as having informed his fellow soldiers that he would write 'anything and everything that will bring in money'.

His gifted biographer, Margaret Lane, makes the point, no doubt rightly, that Edgar Wallace was the best-selling author of all time. He wrote 150 novels in twenty-seven years, in addition to a number of extremely successful plays. He died leaving £140,000 worth of debts. His delights were the turf, the stage and the Press Club, and his frenzied extravagance was of course a compensation for the deprivations of his youth. It was of a piece with his refusal, even after he had achieved success, to help or have any association with the mother who had abandoned him. So too was a revealing statement of his, which Margaret Lane quotes: 'I hate the British working man; I have no sympathy with him; whether he lives or dies, feeds or starves is not of the slightest interest to me.' Not for Wallace the family prayers, the scientific study of agriculture, the service on the bench, though he did, it is true, once stand for Parliament, somewhat improbably and fortunately unsuccessfully, as Liberal candidate for Blackpool.

Something of Wallace's differences in outlook and background from those of Haggard is revealed in the kind of hero he created in his African stories, though the two men's heroes also have significant points in common.

Wallace was sent by Alfred Harmsworth to report for the *Daily Mail* on the treatment of the inhabitants of the Belgian Congo by their rulers, of which some horrifying accounts had appeared in the *Daily Chronicle*. Not long after returning he was fired from the *Daily Mail,* and he then entered a bleak period when he found it extremely difficult to sell any of his work. He had a number of discussions with a Mrs Thorne of the *Weekly Tale-Teller,* to whom he spoke of his experiences in the Congo, and it was at her suggestion that he began to write a series of stories around the character of Mr Commissioner Sanders. In time Wallace developed other leading characters in his African stories, the Army officer Bones and the African Bosambo, but none of them is as memorable a creation as Sanders, or Sandy, of the River.

Sanders is a professional. 'There is one type of man that can rule native provinces wisely, and that type is best represented by Sanders.' He 'knew the native mind much better than any man living. . . . He thought like a native, and there were moments when he acted not unlike a barbarian.' He also acknowledged an order of merit of the various indigenous peoples of the African continent, which is roughly in reverse order of book learning. 'The Zulu were men, the Basuto were men, yet childlike in their grave faith. The black men who wore the fez were subtle, but trustworthy; but the brown men of the Gold Coast, who talked English, wore European clothes, and called one another "Mr" were Sanders' pet abomination.' In particular Sanders has no time for the Reverend Kenneth McDolan, the black missionary.

> 'Get out of that chair,' said Sanders, who had no small talk worth mentioning, 'and stand up when I come out to you.'

Sanders's methods are harsh. Take the education of King Peter of the Isisi for instance.

The king rose reluctantly, and Sanders grabbed him by the scruff of the neck.

Swish!

The cane caught him most undesirably, and he sprang into the air with a yell.

Swish, swish, swish!

. . . This was the beginning of King Peter's education, for thus was he taught obedience.

These methods are certainly efficacious. Before long stories begin to spread of a young king who is a Solomon in judgment, and the king's devotion to Sanders is such that he eventually gives his life for him.

Sanders has a particular aversion to those who come out from England and interfere in one way or another with his administration. There is the Hon. George Teakle, a newspaper correspondent who has got his job because he is the son of the proprietor. There is the misfit who is sent from England with an impressive reputation and who is Sanders's deputy for a time. 'He was a Bachelor of Law, had read Science, and had acquired in a methodical fashion a working acquaintance with Swahili, bacteriology, and medicine.' In a very short time he was 'at home fulfilling the post of assistant examiner in mechanics at South Kensington. . . . and filling in his time with lecturing on "The Migration of the Bantu Races".' Worst of all are the representatives of the Isisi Exploitation Syndicate Ltd, which was 'born between the entrée and the sweet at the house of a gentleman whose Christian name was Isidore, and who lived in Maida Vale'. Isidore's partner 'called himself McPherson every day of the year except on Yum Kippur'. Not even Jacob Meyer comes off as badly as that.

Wallace insisted that in Sanders he had created an unconventional hero. Heroes, he wrote, were expected to be tall and handsome, with flashing eyes, of gentle address and full of soft phrases for women. Sanders was far from tall, he had a yellowish face, and he 'had no use for women any way'. When one of Sanders's young assistants becomes involved with an African girl, Sanders tells him that 'monkey tricks' of that kind may be good enough for the Belgian Congo or Togoland, but they are not good enough for Sanders's 'little strip of wilderness'. Of himself he says that people who describe him as a woman–hater are wrong. He honours women because they suffer torments in childbirth and respects them because they are brave and loyal.

The closest links between the harsh, professional Sanders and Newbolt Man in his purest form is not, however, resistance to the lures of women or even a cultivated philistinism, but dedication to service, and it is a service given wholeheartedly, not only to a crown, but to a system. Wallace himself subscribed unreservedly to that system. Of one of his early books of poems written during his time in South Africa a critic wrote in the *Daily Chronicle:* 'If only he would leave politics and empire and the Royal Family and the British Deity alone for ever!' Nearly thirty years later Arnold Bennett was to write: 'Edgar Wallace has a very grave defect, and I will not hide it. He is content with society as it is. He parades no subversive opinions. He is "correct".'

At the height of his fame Wallace was turning out at prodigious speed one mystery story after another, most of them set in London and the home counties. He created a rich variety of villains and some memorable characters of the racing world. But he never again created such a colourful hero as Sanders, who, however unlovable he may be, must be accorded a distinguished position in the gallery of those characters of English fiction whose place is overseas and whose service is to an empire. Wallace certainly had a particular fondness for the characters from his books about Africa, for the names he gave to the first two racehorses he ever owned were Sanders and Bosambo. Both were consistently unsuccessful and both cost him a great deal of money.

In 1932 Q. D. Leavis published a work of criticism entitled *Fiction and the Reading Public,* in which she essayed to demonstrate, at some length, that popular literature had declined in quali-

ty since Bunyan wrote *The Pilgrim's Progress.* As part of her re-
searches the author sent a questionnaire to a number of well-known
writers and discovered, apparently to her surprise, that several of
them took exception to being described as 'best-selling' novelists.
Among the more colourful of the replies she received came from the
author of *Beau Geste,* P. C. Wren, himself a former *légionnaire.*
Wren informed her that the bulk of his readers were the 'cleanly-
minded, virile, outdoor sort', and that he himself, although he
made large sums of money by writing, was neither a professional
novelist nor a 'long-haired literary cove'. Of his publishers he
wrote that the late Sir John Murray and others were sportsmen
and gentlemen who had 'somehow strayed into the muddy paths
of commerce, and somehow contrived to remain sportsmen and
gentlemen and jolly good business men as well'. It is tempting to
think that Wren was pulling Mrs Leavis's leg, but I doubt whether
he was.

Wren had the distinction of being the first man to convey to
readers of popular English fiction a convincing picture of life in
the French Foreign Legion: the boredom, the corruption, the heat,
the drinking, the pride in personal appearance, above all the pride
in the legion. The authenticity tends to flag somewhat in the
dialogue passages. An American, who has himself done quite a
stretch in the desert, says to his 'pard': ' "Say, son Hank, don't go
and fall in love with that li'll peach, or I shall hand in my checks
and wilt to the bone-orchard." ' But the flow of the narrative does
not suffer unduly in consequence.

Wren's heroes are fighting men. There is, for instance, Henri de
Beaujolais in *Beau Sabreur,* who had an English mother and won
the senior quarter-mile at Eton. He becomes the youngest major
in the French Army, even though everything in his make-up, so
far as national characteristics are concerned, suggests that the
maternal influence was dominant. The preface to *Beau Sabreur*
appropriately includes Newbolt's lines:

To count the life of battle good,
And clear the land that gave you birth,

Bring nearer yet the brotherhood
That binds the brave of all the earth.

There is a lot of 'David and Jonathan', 'tremendous attraction' and 'strongest liking at first sight' in the relationship between Beaujolais and the subaltern d'Auray de Redon, but it is not of course expressed in the language of the long-haired literary coves, whom Wren probably both feared and distrusted.

Two of Wren's heroes who may be thought to reveal more of his feelings and of his attitude to society than most appear in *The Wages of Virtue,* which he wrote in 1913 and which was published three years later. These are an older and a younger man, who complement each other in a manner not unlike that of Rider Haggard's characters.

The older hero is Sir Montague Merline, whose wife has fallen in love with his friend and safari companion in East Africa, Lord Huntington. 'If,' Wren asks, 'living in Mayfair and falling in love with your neighbour's wife, the correct thing to do is to go and shoot lions in East Africa, is it, conversely, the correct thing to go and live in Mayfair if, shooting lions in East Africa, you fall in love with your neighbour's wife?' It is this sort of aside which creates, momentarily at least, the doubt whether Wren was or was not pulling Mrs Leavis's leg.

Lord Huntington's problem is at least partially solved by a report that Sir Montague has been killed, but in fact, after having had a bullet in his head and losing and recovering his memory, Sir Montague has joined the Foreign Legion under the name of John Bull. There we find him as

the grey Jean Boule, so old, so young, doyen of Legionaires, so quick, strong, skilful and enduring at *la boxe* . . . watching with a contemptuous smile some mixed and messy fighting . . . between an Alsatian and an Italian, in which the Italian kicked his opponent in the stomach and partly ate his ear, and the Alsatian used his hands solely for the purpose of throttling. Why couldn't they stand up and fight like gentlemen under Queensberry rules?

The younger hero, who calls himself Reginald Rupert but who is in fact Lord Huntington's son, also joins the Foreign Legion. He is 'straight as a lance, thin, very broad in the shoulders and narrow of waist and hip; apparently as clean and unruffled as when leaving his golf-club pavilion [*sic*] for a round on the links; cool, self-possessed, haughty, aristocratic and clean-cut of feature'. He stands out among the other new recruits 'like a Derby winner among a string of equine ruins', serving to emphasize that 'breed is a very remarkable thing, even more distinctive than race'.

The two Englishmen are understandably drawn to each other. Rupert addresses Légionnaire John Bull as 'sir' and when asked why he does so replies: ' "Because you are senior and a Sahib, I suppose." ' John Bull for his part is delighted to find Rupert is genuinely keen on soldiering and tells him: ' "I have had unlimited experience of active service of all kinds, against enemies of all sorts except Europeans, and I hope to have that—against Germany—before I have gone." '

There are some minor plots, one of them concerning the principal bully and braggart, a Neapolitan music-hall wrestler named Luigi. Luigi's girl, Carmelita, has served him devotedly, even to the point of working as a prostitute in Marseilles when he was short of funds. Her nature, we learn, 'was essentially virginal, delicate and of crystal purity'. But in spite of this, as John Bull says of Luigi, ' "the swine's carrying on at the same time with Madame la Cantinière" '.

' "What's his particular line of nastiness—besides cheating women I mean?" ' Rupert asks. John Bull explains that Luigi is ' "the Ultimate Bounder . . . the Complete Cad, and the Finished Bully" '.

There is a curious interlude, which Wren states is based on fact, when it is discovered that two Russian recruits who claim to be brothers are in fact brother and sister. The danger to the sister at the hands of Luigi is obvious, and John Bull wonders whether a combined force consisting of himself, Rupert, a Cockney known as Erbiggins, an American, the girl's brother and ' "perhaps one or two of the more decent foreigners, such as Hans Djoolte and old Tant–de–Soif," ' could ' "ensure her a decent life free from molestation and annoyance" '. But he abandons the hope and realizes the girl will have to escape. (Hans Djoolte is a Dutchman who follows the example of Arthur in *Tom Brown's School Days* by kneeling down and publicly saying his prayers. On this issue the English–speaking legionaries combine effectively to prevent Luigi from exacting punishment.)

All this is conventional. Where more revealing insight comes is when we learn that Reginald Rupert hopes, before his father dies, to have been in many armies and frontier police forces, to have been a sailor, cowboy, trapper, explorer, and so on.

> He hoped to continue to turn up in any part of the world where there was a war. What Reginald, like his father, loathed and feared was Modern Society life, and in fact all civilised life as it had presented itself to his eyes—with its incredibly false standards, values and ideals, its shoddy shams and vulgar pretences, its fat indulgences, slothfulness and folly.

Newbolt Man cast in the role, not of the upholder of the social order, but of rebel against what is considered its decadence was a new figure, of whom more would be heard after the war of 1914-18.

Rider Haggard was a better prose artist than P. C. Wren and a much more gifted weaver of adventure stories, but both men depended for their effects to a comparable extent on their first–hand knowledge of the African continent. In their wake came a flood of writers, all depicting a contemporary overseas scene more or less convincingly, all telling tales of adventure, and all presenting to the reader a hero or heroes cast in a mould now familiar enough to be reassuring.

India provided the settings used by a number of popular women novelists. The best known of these was probably Maud Diver, who even contrived to find her young Englishmen living in India romantic. (She did herself marry a subaltern.) 'The much-abused public-school product *in excelsis,*' she wrote in *The Singer Passes.*

> No parade of brains or force; revelling in understatement; but they've got guts, those boys, and a fine sense of responsibility. . . . They're no thinkers, but they're born improvisers and administrators. They've just sauntered down the ages, impervious to darts of criticism or hate or jealousy.

In the same work, which was published in 1934, describing the individual specimen, she wrote of 'the vital force, the pluck, endurance and irresistible spirit of enterprise, which, it has been aptly said, make him, at his best, the most romantic figure of our modern time'. The Englishmen's qualities are duly recognized by Indians too. In another of Maud Diver's novels, published four years later, three Indian officers of different religious faiths take part in a shooting contest and decide, in order to ensure fair play, that the scores must be kept by a 'pukka British officer'.

The treaty ports and other Chinese-speaking areas in which Europeans were established also provided plenty of scope for adventure. In *The River Pirates,* for instance, Herbert Strang, an industrious artisan of a writer—or, to be exact, two writers working in collaboration—who had something in common with Percy F. Westerman, showed how two young Englishmen could outwit a variety of bloodthirsty enemies, including a band of Chinese pirates and a sinister and powerful Russian named Mirski. The author insists moreover that his heroes are in no way exceptional.

> The only human beings to be seen on the water-front were two tallish youths whose features and complexions showed them to be neither Portuguese nor Chinamen. They were ruddy, brown-haired, grey-eyed, like thousands of boys who may be seen on the playing-fields of English public schools.

The boys, who are brothers, are barely distinguishable from each other in character except that Michael, who is the elder, tends to take command and Larry, the younger, can operate a wireless transmitter. Their achievements are particularly remarkable in that, though continually involved in fighting, they seem to need no more lethal weapons than the butts of shot–guns. Nor do they receive much outside help, though they do, it is true, have a 'boy' called Ah Sung, who is good at stowing baggage or, as he puts it, making 'evelyting all plopa'. There is not a single female character in the book.

During the period of more than sixty years between the publication of *King Solomon's Mines* and the death of Maud Diver in 1945 another genre of novel, differing in setting from what may reasonably be called the Rider Haggard school, also enjoyed great popularity. In this the adventures take place, not against a closely observed African or Asian background, but in a country of the imagination. Of all the imaginary countries of English popular fiction the most famous is Anthony Hope's Ruritania.

The sub–title of *The Prisoner of Zenda* is *The history of three months in the life of an English gentleman.* Anthony Hope's hero, Rudolf Rassendyll, is in fact a nobleman, being the younger brother of the Earl of Burlesdon and related by blood through a union out of wedlock to the Elphbergs, the ruling house of Ruritania. It is the physical resemblance arising out of the relationship which enables Rassendyll to impersonate the king.

Rassendyll is unfailingly chivalrous, but he is certainly not sex-less. 'I am not a slow–blooded man, and I had not kissed Princess Flavia's cheek for nothing.' His sister–in–law complains of his idle-ness, but he brushes this aside by informing the reader that her family is hardly of the same standing as the Rassendylls and saying to his sister–in–law: 'Our family doesn't need to do things.' He does indulge in that playing down of the emotions which readily results in understatement: he believes he is unlikely to survive the final attack on the castle which is to lead to the rescue of the king, and in analyzing his sensations before going into action records: 'My predominant feeling was, neither anxiety for the King nor longing for Flavia, but an intense desire to smoke.' But he has neither the philistinism nor the anti–intellectual bias of Newbolt Man. This is not altogether surprising, for his creator, Anthony Hope Hawkins, was a man of first–class intellect, a Balliol scholar with firsts in mods and greats and president of the Oxford Union before being called to the bar.

In *Rupert of Hentzau,* the sequel to *The Prisoner of Zenda,* there is rather more emphasis on Rassendyll's peculiarly English qualities, for the narrator now is not Rassendyll himself, but old Fritz von Tarlenheim, the Queen's chamberlain, who can observe Englishmen from the outside. 'Danger and the need for action acted on him like a draught of good wine on a seasoned drinker. He was not only himself, but more than himself, the indolence that marred him in quiet hours sloughed off.' Later 'Rudolf's excitement left him as suddenly as it had come; he was again the cool, shrewd, nonchalant Englishman'. In *Rupert of Hentzau* Rassendyll is given a servant, James, who uncomplainingly undergoes dangers solely out of loyalty to his employer. This was a figure who was to become increasingly familiar to readers in the 1920s, when former batmen, in fiction at least, remained after demobilization in the service of their former officers. James, though described as 'a little man' and addressed by Colonel Sapt as 'Mr Valet', is not only courageous but has some of the resourcefulness of a Jeeves. But Rassendyll himself, even as seen by Fritz von Tarlenheim, has only a few of the essential ingredients of Newbolt Man. If not Ruritania itself, certainly the other imaginary countries which Ruritania spawned were better suited as backgrounds to romance as the motion picture industry understood the term than to that in which Rider Haggard used it. For Newbolt Man himself countries to be found on the map tended to be more appropriate settings than countries to be found only in the mind.

Anthony Hope demonstrated how the narrative could be brilliantly sustained in a story of adventure with a hero differing happily from the stereotype. In *The Four Feathers* A. E. W. Mason showed how the best and worst features of Newbolt Man, in the hero himself and in others, could shape the life of a character created with a depth and realism which no stereotype could ever attain.

The Four Feathers is, on the surface at least, a novel of overseas adventure, and Mason himself was a man who both sought adventure and was well equipped to cope with it when it came. Actor, playwright as well as novelist, war-time officer in the Royal Marines, actively engaged in secret service work in Spain, Morocco and Mexico, he found recreation in exploring, sailing and mountaineering. He was a gifted raconteur, and Reginald Pound, editor of the *Strand* magazine, wrote of him that he had the air of having enjoyed the good life 'to the last drop—yachts, House of Commons, plentiful travel, a country house, the Garrick Club, and any number of devoted friends'. Mason even succeeded, where other novelists failed, in being returned as a Liberal Member of Parliament. (Anthony Hope Hawkins was yet another unsuccessful Liberal candidate. He is also believed to have been one of those on whom King George V would have been advised to confer peerages if no other way had been found of persuading the House of Lords to accept parliamentary reform.)

With this background Mason might have been expected in the climate of the time in which he wrote—*The Four Feathers* was first published in 1902—to create heroes who sauntered through all dangers unflinchingly. In fact the hero of *The Four Feathers*, Harry Feversham, is a man with doubts, particularly doubts about his own courage in the face of physical danger. He is the son of a general and comes of a family in which such doubts are not entertained. 'Personal courage and an indomitable self-confidence were the chief, indeed the only qualities which sprang to light in General Feversham.'

The only one of General Feversham's friends who has any insight into Harry's character is a retired naval officer, Lieutenant Sutch. The others are 'lean-faced men, hard as iron, rugged in feature, thin-lipped, with firm chins and straight level mouths, narrow foreheads, and the steel-blue inexpressive eyes . . . men rather stupid—all of them, in a word, first-class fighting men, but not one of them a first-class soldier.' Sutch was in love with Harry's mother, who is now dead, and he sees in the son 'his mother's dark and haunted eyes, his mother's breadth of forehead, his mother's delicacy of profile, his mother's imagination'.

Harry Feversham becomes engaged to an Irish girl, Ethne Eustace. With the prospect of matrimony it would have been permissible, according to the code of the time, for him to resign his commission in the Army in order to look after her estates. In fact he resigns on receiving a telegram informing him that his regiment is to be sent to Egypt for active service. This is discovered by three of his fellow officers, each of whom sends him a white feather. Ethne Eustace, on hearing what has happened, adds a fourth.

For a time Sutch is virtually the only human being to whom Harry can talk, and Sutch compares him with Hamlet.

> The thing which he foresaw, which he thought over, which he imagined in the act and in the consequence—that he shrinks from, upbraiding himself even as you have done. Yet when the moment of action comes, sharp and immediate, does he fail? No, he excels, and just by reason of that foresight.

Sutch believes Harry's mother would have understood his predicament, but that few other women would, certainly not Ethne. Harry defends Ethne with the explanation, which is true so far as it goes, that he was defrauding her into marriage.

The first act of courage on Harry's part which impresses Sutch is his decision to beard his father and tell him just what he has done and why. Here Mason deals very fairly with the general, who does not understand Harry's motives, but who refrains from punishing his son by cutting off his allowance. Harry Feversham's other instances of courage follow. Through a series of actions performed in the Sudan, in which he is on his own, with no troops to support him, and faces not simply dangers but prolonged physical suffering, Harry, who has carefully hoarded the white feathers, obliges the three officers in turn to take them back. Finally he confronts Ethne, who is aware of how much he has changed.

> There had been a timidity in his manner in those days, a peculiar diffidence, a continual expectation of other men's contempt, which had gone from him. He was now quietly self-possessed; not arrogant; on the other hand, not diffident. He had put himself to a long, hard test; and he knew that he had not failed.

The secondary hero of the book, Colonel Jack Durrance, who rowed in the same college boat at Oxford as Harry, has a more conventional career as a soldier until he is blinded, when he says of himself: ' "I am not clever. I can't sit in a chair and amuse myself by thinking, not having any intellect to buck about. I have lived out of doors and hard, and that's the only sort of life that suits me." ' Yet there is a delicacy in Durrance too which is not far below the surface. 'Sympathy had stood Durrance in the stead of much ability', and he is promoted ahead of more apparently able men, not least because of his understanding of the 'sorely harassed' tribes of the eastern Sudan. Durrance was

> a soldier of a type not so rare as the makers of war stories wish their readers to believe. Hector of Troy was his ancestor; he was neither hysterical in his language nor vindictive in his acts; he was not an elderly school-boy with a taste for loud talk, but a quiet man who did his work without noise; who could be stern when occasion needed and of an unflinching severity; but whose nature was gentle and compassionate.

Perhaps Newbolt Man does emerge here to some extent, but it is in a rare, three-dimensional form. It was not the least of Mason's distinctions that in *The Four Feathers* he was able to achieve characterization in depth without sacrifice of that skill in story-telling which was so evident a quality in so many English writers of novels of adventure during a period of more than half a century. How nearly, as a result, *The Four Feathers* comes to meriting inclusion within the category of the great English novels must be a question of opinion. Some seventy years after its publication it is still, to me at least, supremely satisfying reading.

CHAPTER SEVEN

Detectives, Secret Agents and Demobilized Officers

Few writers were better equipped by personal interests and inclinations to create Newbolt Man in fiction than Arthur Conan Doyle. As a young man he served aboard a whaler which sailed from Peterhead to the Arctic. He was a pioneer of skiing as an international sport and is reputed to have introduced Norwegian skis into Switzerland. He established the first rifle club in Hindhead on his own property, he drove round the Brooklands racing circuit at 100 miles an hour at the age of seventy, and in 1903 he told P. G. Wodehouse he would like to be a parachutist. After the South African war he drew up plans for a national militia in which he emphasized the importance of the amateur, stating fairly enough: 'Our professional soldiers have not shown that they were endowed with clear vision.' He was a man of exceptional physical strength and weighed over seventeen stone.

A number of Doyle's historical characters are indeed specimens of Newbolt Man, but this is certainly not true of his most famous creation, Sherlock Holmes. Doyle gave Holmes something of his physical strength and a masterful personality. There were resemblances too between the attitudes of hero and creator towards women. Holmes is immune to passion or any strong feelings towards women. He does admire Irene Adler, but only, we are assured, because she proved his equal in quickness of wit and decisiveness of action. Doyle formed an attachment to a young woman when he was twenty–three, but, in the words of his biographer, Pierre Nordon, 'he was still, and remained for a long time afterwards, too much of a bachelor by inclination for any woman to play a significant part in his life'.

Unlike Newbolt Man, however, Holmes is an intellectual and something of an aesthete. He has a 'cold, precise, but admirably balanced mind'. He is a drug–taker, 'alternating from week to week between cocaine and ambition, the drowsiness of the drug and the fierce energy of his own keen nature'. He is not only a violinist but a composer of some merit. He reads Petrarch and Horace, Goethe and Meredith. When he took to the profession of detective 'the stage lost a fine actor, even as science lost an acute reasoner'. Dr Watson, whom Desmond MacCarthy described as the most re-presentative Englishman of his period, may be thought to belong more to the tradition of Newbolt Man. Watson saw military service in Afghanistan; he is always ready to arm himself with his service revolver when Holmes considers the dangers warrant it; and his loyalty to Holmes the leader is unquestionable. Moreover he has a mediocre mind. ('I trust that I am not more dense than my neighbours.') But Watson is a foil, and it is Holmes who is the hero.

Doyle's presentation of Holmes as an intellectual no doubt stemmed in part from the fascination he felt for Dr Joseph Bell, the Edinburgh surgeon on whom the character of Holmes was initially based. But he was also sufficiently perceptive and sensitive an artist to appreciate that criminal detection, when carried out by an amateur, is an intellectual exercise. Sherlock Holmes has proved indestructible, but, as is well known, Doyle himself repeatedly felt the urge to destroy him. It was an urge which may well have been prompted by a feeling of being less at home and less in sympathy with an intellectual hero than with, for example, Sir Nigel Loring. Perhaps there was more of Doyle in Dr Watson than it is nowadays fashionable to concede.

That an amateur detective, to be convincing, must depend mainly on his powers of reasoning was a discovery which had already been made by Edgar Allan Poe. Other later masters of the genre understood this too. Hercule Poirot with his little grey cells, the shrewd old lady Miss Marple, Margery Allingham's unashamedly intellectual Albert Campion, Father Brown, the priest with a perception of the truth of paradox, all solve their problems by observation and reasoning while eschewing violence. (G. K. Chesterton's Father Brown is so unlike Newbolt Man that his features could well be described as 'unclear–cut'.)

To less gifted writers of detective stories the need to equip their heroes with convincing intellectual powers was not so apparent. But the personalities of Holmes and Watson, and the two men's relationship to each other, made such a deep impact on the reading public that almost inevitably their superficial characteristics were continually reproduced. The less original the imitators, the more readily they grafted these characteristics on to the stereotype of a popular hero, i.e. a simplified version of Newbolt Man. One outcome of this process was Sexton Blake.

Sexton Blake, the detective, flourished in the magazines of Harmsworth's Amalgamated Press for many years. According to E. S. Turner more than a hundred authors wrote Sexton Blake stories, producing between them some two million words. The Sexton Blake industry seems to have been established in 1893, the year following the publication of *The Adventures of Sherlock Holmes*. After a time Blake was forced to migrate from his earlier habitat to Baker Street; when faced with seductive adventuresses he is known as a 'synonym for austerity'; and he even writes 'monographs'. His strength, however, lies not in reasoning but in action, and the British nation evidently owed him a debt when he refused the Kaiser's offer to appoint him head of the German secret service. Kindred spirits to Sexton Blake were Nelson Lee and Dixon Brett and Falcon Swift. All belonged to a type educated at public schools—Sexton Blake, it seems, attended several—as well as Oxford or Cambridge (or both) and blues were conferred on them with some prodigality.

Rather over forty years after the publication of *The Adventures of Sherlock Holmes*, H. C. McNeile, who wrote under the name of 'Sapper', published in book form a number of stories with the title *Ronald Standish*. Standish is, like Holmes, an amateur detective who handles only cases which interest him. Like Holmes too he is continually able to outwit the police, who even forty years after the days of Inspector Lestrade have plenty to learn. 'At times some new man was apt to smile contemptuously at the presumption of an amateur pitting himself against the official force, but the smile generally faded before long.' Standish is also endowed with 'an astounding memory' and 'powers of observation to a very marked degree'. But in spite of all this he 'seemed the last person in the world to become a detective'. He is 'a born player of games, wealthy and distinctly good–looking'. When expecting a visit from an 'extremely pretty' girl he says: '"Let us, therefore, endeavour to make the darned place a little more presentable to the female optic"', and duly throws a couple of niblicks in a corner and removes a cricket bat from a chair. (The girls in these stories fall into two categories, the 'extremely pretty' and the 'delightfully pretty'. Otherwise they are indistinguishable.) One typical setting for an exercise in detection by Standish is a country house, where a party has assembled to play cricket the next day against the Free Foresters. Another is the ancestral home or 'hovel' of 'the dear old Duke of Dorset known to most of the dear old schoolfellows as Catface'.

Standish and Catface seem to have identical views on the conduct expected of Catface's chauffeur.

> 'From what you tell me, Williams is not the sort of man who would play the fool with a girl.'
> 'Most emphatically not,' said the Duke.

Standish has, of course, his attendant Boswell or Watson, a colourless member of the various sporting teams named Bob Miller.

The Holmes–Watson relations and the Holmes–Watson experiences also served as models for heroes whose exercises in deduction were minimal. In Dr Fu–Manchu Sax Rohmer created a character whose villainy, the reader is continually assured, is on a colossal scale. Its purpose remains curiously ill-defined, but we know at least that he is 'the "Yellow Peril" incarnate in one man'. Opium dens of the kind depicted in Conan Doyle's *The Man with the Twisted Lip* are a ready-made background for some of Fu-Manchu's activities, and he uses animals and even vegetables for homicidal purposes with a prodigality exceeding anything recorded in *The Speckled Band*. In one volume of stories alone Fu-Manchu attempts murders through the agencies of a cat, a snake, a baboon and a fungus.

The narrator of the struggle against Fu-Manchu is Dr Petrie, whose medical practice is not so extensive as to preclude him from taking part in adventure when it calls. The hero whose doings Dr Petrie chronicles is Nayland Smith, 'the gaunt, bronzed and steely-eyed Burmese commissioner', who has a masterful voice and 'sinews like piano-wires'. (' "Smith!" I cried. "Smith, old man, by God, I'm glad to see you." ')

Nayland Smith is able to 'commandeer' a stranger's car 'on a matter of life and death'. He has 'the British Government behind him in all that he might choose to do', and he is 'vested with powers to silence the press'. But even with these advantages and confronting the Chinese doctor, as he does, in a home rather than an away tie, he still has to be on his guard against seductive women.

> 'A woman made a fool of me once,' [he says], 'but I learned my lesson; you have failed to learn yours. If you are determined to go to pieces on the rock that broke up Adam, do so! But don't involve me in the wreck, Petrie, for that might mean a yellow emperor of the world.'

Petrie, like Watson, is slightly susceptible to the attractions of what is still known as 'the fair sex'.

Largely because he was not an intellectual, and could never be convincingly presented as one, Newbolt Man tended to persist in the guise of a detective only in works of minimal literary merit. Where he succeeded most convincingly in the post-Holmes era was in a different kind of popular story. In this, suspense and mystery, crime and disguise are all to be found, but the hero himself depends much more on quick reactions and an instinct for self–preservation than he does on logical reasoning. The generally accepted name for this kind of story changed gradually from 'shocker' to 'thriller'.

John Buchan was said to have been induced by A. J. Balfour's admiration of the 'shockers' of E. Phillips Oppenheim to try to write something in the same vein himself. The extent to which Buchan studied Oppenheim as a master remains unclear, but in so far as he did he must surely have appreciated the practised skill acquired and developed by a writer who was unswervingly a professional.

Oppenheim retired from his family's leather business in Leicester to become a full–time writer, but even while he was still actively employed in the business he published thirteen full–length books in four years. The total volume of his output has been estimated at more than sixteen times the length of the Bible. In the words of his biographer, Robert Standish, Oppenheim 'drew his characters in the likeness of what he believed his readers would like themselves to be'. A high proportion of these characters are princes and princesses, and between them they command the services of a welter of *maîtres d'hotel.*

Of Oppenheim's heroes two in particular show how skilfully he adapted himself to the demands of what was already an established tradition. Oppenheim did not have the kind of background and personal inclinations which enabled so many writers to create Newbolt Man in one form or another largely by looking into themselves. His family was middle–class, but it was manufacturing not professional middle–class. He had a Germanic, not a traditionally English surname; he did not go to either Oxford or Cambridge; and so far was he from shunning the company of women that the yacht he kept moored off the south coast of France was commonly known as the 'floating double–bed', and he seems to have combined a marriage, which both partners found deeply enriching, with fairly persistent infidelities. Nevertheless, once we are introduced to Major Henry Owston, the hero and narrator of *The Treasure House of Martin Hews,* we know we are on familiar ground.

Owston is 6 feet 3½ inches tall. He 'won all the prizes worth taking' in the Oxford v. Cambridge athletics match eighteen years ago. He was in the semi-finals of the amateur boxing championship six years after that. He was considered good enough to play county cricket, 'even for Yorkshire', but the war of 1914-18 intervened. In that war he was awarded the D.S.O. and was twice mentioned in despatches. After the war he soldiered for a time in Morocco with the Spaniards and killed a Frenchman in circumstances which were never revealed. All this we learn from Martin Hews, Owston's prospective employer, a villainous cripple, who is reading from Owston's dossier. Owston would have been too modest to reveal it all himself.

When Owston takes service with Martin Hews he is penniless. He is, he explains, still ' "a member of the Rag . . . rather a matter of kindly sufferance, I am afraid. . . . I am supposed to be out of England." ' Later he explains: ' "A man who has been rescued from starvation, or from borrowing from his friends—which is a trifle worse—isn't very particular what he does so long as it's on the level." ' The job Owston is given is to protect his employer against a gang headed by a master of disguises named Joseph, who is determined to deprive Hews of the treasure he has unlawfully acquired. After a certain amount of fighting Hews sums Owston up as 'a brave man, dogged of purpose, not over-intelligent, but with sufficient brains to adapt himself to a difficult situation'. He then asks whether he knows much about women. Owston, in spite of being familiar with the 'bazaars of Constantinople' as well as with Naples and Marseilles, replies: 'Not a damned thing.' He corrects himself, thinking his language may have been intemperate, and adds: 'I know very little about them—haven't come my way somehow.'

Joseph has a girl friend, a sexy young Jewess named Rachel, who is herself attracted to Owston, and Hews suggests that Owston should take advantage of this attraction to obtain information about Joseph. On hearing this Owston's 'first impulse was towards blasphemy', but he calms down by counting ten and quietly refuses the assignment. Rachel, after complaining of Owston's failure to be 'a bit more pally', offers in effect what Hews requires, but Owston's resistance is unyielding. He tells Rachel he is convinced 'your mission here is to vamp me *à la cinéma*', and adds that he is unlikely to learn anything himself because 'girls are too good sports to give their sweethearts away for nothing'.

Rachel is not the only girl with whom Owston in confronted. There is also Hews's niece, Beatrice Essiter. After a time Owston begins to realize that 'although she seemed indifferent to, almost contemptuous of, the fact, she was really an unusually beautiful young woman'. Nevertheless he says of her to a friend of his, a Scotland Yard inspector: '"She's inclined to be supercilious, she is undoubtedly fastidious, she is not in the least nervous, has plenty of courage, and I should think she'd make a brave fight anywhere."' In fact Beatrice is human enough, and quite enough of a bitch, to aim some pretty telling swipes at Rachel, describing her at one point as 'that most enslaving young woman from Shoreditch'. Towards the end of the book Beatrice inherits two fortunes. By then Owston, for better or for worse, has married her.

In *The Million Pound Deposit,* which appeared in 1930, a year after publication of *The Treasure House of Martin Hews,* Oppenheim did create an industrial background of a kind, although it is only lightly sketched in. A formula has been stolen from a firm manufacturing artificial silk in Leeds. The fortunes of the firm were built by the first Lord Dutley, and the hero of the book is his son Charles, who, when he is not shooting lions in Abyssinia, lives in 'a pleasant little bachelor Mayfair residence'. Charles, the second Baron Dutley, worked in the business for a year or two, left it to serve in the 1914-18 war, and took no further part in its affairs until the theft of the formula occurred. It is at this point that the managing director, Sir Matthew Parkinson, who has treated him as a figurehead, first begins to realize he has underrated him.

> The two presented a curious contrast—the stalwart York-
> shireman, a splendid figure of a man in his towering height
> and strength, his broad, benevolent face and features as though
> cut out of granite, and Dutley, in his fashionably cut but well-
> worn riding clothes, his sunburnt complexion, his clear blue eyes,
> and the half-gentle, half-humorous curve of his lips. By the side
> of Sir Matthew, he appeared almost insignificant, yet a physiog-
> nomist might have remarked upon the fact that, small though
> the chin was, it had a firm setting, and though he had never
> quite got rid of his Oxford drawl, his words were crisply and
> definitely spoken. . . . Eton and Oxford had set their mark
> upon him, and the type was strange to the sturdy, little-travelled
> Yorkshireman.

Dutley has a manservant named Burdett, who, on hearing there is a new prospect of danger, groans, but only 'in spirit'. He has, after all, had nine months in Abyssinia, which he disliked, and barely three days in London, which he loves. 'Well-trained servant though he was, his face fell.' Training of course tells, and before long Burdett is saying:

> 'If this business is going to lead to any scrapping, hadn't
> I better stick close, and let Mrs Bulwell and Robert look after
> the house? We've got out of a good many tight corners together,
> my lord, but it's needed two of us sometimes.'

Dutley, like Major Owston, is faced with a choice between two girls. He is officially engaged to one named Lucille, who is a being of a kind once known as a 'bright young thing' and who is more than ready to ditch him when she learns that his family business may be on the rocks. As an alternative there is Grace, the daughter of Sir Matthew Parkinson, whom Dutley has known since she was a child, and who has grown into a 'slim, graceful figure, adorably neat in her simple but elegant clothes, and fashionable little hat'. After a certain amount of Grace's company Dutley confesses:

> 'I am a commonplace young man, and there are some things which don't appeal to me. By this time in the evening, Lucille has smoked so many cigarettes and drunk so many cocktails, that indigestion with her has become a habit.'

Grace joins Dutley as an ally in tracking down the criminals who have stolen the formula, and she is impressed by what she considers a new firmness in him. Only once before did she know him to be equally firm. This was, when captaining the Yorkshire Gentlemen, he refused to put on a bowler whose action he questioned. Dutley explains quietly:

> 'The fellow threw. . . . We wanted to win, but we didn't want to cheat.'

Cricket in fact plays an important part in the discovery of the criminals, for their leader is an Old Harrovian, who had been taking wickets in the Eton v. Harrow match when Dutley came in and hit the first ball he received from him into the pavilion. After that the future criminal lost his length. He also never forgave Dutley.

Even after the criminals have been unmasked there is some concern about how the company's shareholders will react. Again Dutley is equal to the occasion.

> 'Have you ever, by chance, Mr Cooke,' he enquired, 'met face to face an angry rhinoceros, who is very hungry, who has lost his wife, and whom you have had the misfortune to slightly wound?'
>
> 'I have not,' the Solicitor admitted.
>
> 'Well, I have,' Dutley confided, rising to his feet, 'and I'm not going to be afraid of any shareholders.'

Oppenheim knew what his readers wanted, and he gave it to them, including heroes whose very charms derived largely from their familiarity. There may be little that is new or original in either Major Owston or the second Baron Dutley, but as figures cast from a mould they have a flawlessness which only a skilled craftsman could achieve.

Edgar Wallace was the one writer of thrillers who could command a readership comparable with that of Oppenheim, and he too understood what was expected of the heroes of such books in the 1920s. As a newspaper reporter Wallace had plenty of first-hand knowledge of the kind of man who was likely to become a detective inspector in real life. Yet he could still create characters such as Jimmy Sepping in *The Missing Million,* which was first published in 1923, and Dick Gordon in *The Fellowship of the Frog,* which came out a year later.

Dick or Captain Gordon 'was thirty and looked eighteen, with his smooth, boyish face'. The Foreign Secretary has asked him to 'supplement the ordinary police protection', adding by way of explanation: ' "It is a little outside your duties, but your Intelligence work during the war must be my excuse." ' Socially Gordon belongs to a different world from that of his assistant Elk, whose promotion is continually barred by his ignorance of history, and when it comes to a scrap Gordon is seen at his best, largely because he so evidently enjoys it.

Dick Gordon, conspicuously bandaged about the head, something of his good looks spoiled by three latitudinal scratches which ran down [*sic*] his face, sat in his dressing-gown and slippers, a big pipe clenched between his teeth, the picture of battered contentment.

Dick Gordon falls in love with a girl named Ella, who 'conveyed to him an impression of aloofness'. He also observes in her 'a graciousness of carriage, an inspiring refinement of manner'. Ella has a strong sense of the proprieties. When her brother asks her if she is in love with Gordon she replies: ' "That is the kind of question that a gentleman does not ask in such a tone, not even of his sister." ' But for all her prissiness she has a remarkable hold over the master criminal known as the Frog, who controls a vast organization threatening the security of the nation. The Frog is determined to marry Ella—nothing less will do—and this is largely the cause of his downfall. "'I want you! Not now"—he raised his hand as he saw the terror rising in her face. "You shall come to me willingly. . . . Will you marry me, Ella?" She shook her head.' Dick Gordon's courting of Ella is more successful, but in its different way it is of course equally considerate.

Detective Inspector Jimmy Sepping in *The Missing Million* was educated at Oxford. (Both Wallace and Oppenheim preferred Oxford to Cambridge for the backgrounds of their heroes.) While at the university he had a friend named Rex, who has a sister named Joan. Joan is eight years younger that Jimmy, and when Jimmy meets her after a gap of some years he puts his hand on her shoulder as he used to do when she was a child. Suddenly he feels awkward.

> 'Jimmy, you're scared of me?' she challenged.
> 'I am,' he admitted.
> 'Well, don't be.'

Another girl in the book is Donna. She is beautiful and, though at one time given to crime, has become a reformed character through the love of a good man. Knowing she is in extreme danger, she asks Jimmy if she can spend the night in his flat.

> 'Sleep here?' he said in surprise. 'My dear girl, there are no women in this house: I suppose you realize that?'
> 'Can I sit up and talk then?' she asked desperately.

It is hardly surprising that she feels desperate, particularly when Jimmy suggests that she should stay in the flat while he moves to a hotel. She has, after all, come to him for protection. In the end a compromise is reached, with Donna lying fully dressed in the sitting-room and a settee being pulled into a passage and wedged against the sitting-room door. Jimmy's valet, Albert, who is as usual in the danger zone, stands guard, for some reason, over the settee. When a Mills bomb explodes in the flat all three happen fortunately to have taken up positions where they are out of harm's way. Equally fortunately, when a number of policemen and firemen reach the scene of the explosion, they are so preoccupied with their work that they accept Donna's presence as natural, and one of them refers to Donna as Mrs Sepping. Jimmy 'did not trouble to correct the error'.

Edgard Wallace not only knew what his readers wanted. He also knew what they were prepared *en masse* to accept in the private lives of heroes. On the subject of what a later age would call permissiveness he once made, in an address to the Worshipful Company of Stationers, the shrewd comment: 'I like to write stories which contain nothing more than a little innocent murdering.'

As a writer of thrillers John Buchan was not nearly so prolific as either Wallace or Oppenheim. Nor would he have wished to be, for he did not regard himself as altogether a professional writer. He even warned Hugh Walpole against becoming a whole-time man of letters with the comment: 'I love writers individually, but assembled in bulk they affect me with overpowering repugnance.' Nevertheless, while retaining as nearly as he could his amateur status, he brought new qualities to the thriller, qualities which may be thought to have raised it to a new level of excellence. Most of these qualities derived directly from his own personality, some from the company he kept, and like virtually everything Buchan did they brought him exceptional success.

Buchan was listed in *Who's Who* while he was still an undergraduate at Oxford. He became, in the words of Franklin D. Roosevelt, 'the best Governor-General that Canada ever had'. These achievements were in no way attributable to family privilege, though his background was in fact one from which he gained and retained a great deal. He was the son of a minister in the Free Church of Scotland and while still a youth was taking a Sunday School class of boys from the Gorbals. He became an elder of

St Columba's, the Church of Scotland church in Pont Street, London, in 1912, and in 1933, when addressing the General Assembly of the Church of Scotland as Lord High Commissioner, he could say: 'I am one of yourselves, and I have in my bones the tradition of Scottish Presbyterianism.' A sense of purpose and self–reliance were qualities which he revealed early. A contemporary of his at Glasgow University wrote: 'He had an air of simple and convincing assurance. . . . He could depend on himself and others felt that they could depend on him too.'

In these respects Buchan had much in common with Ballantyne, but he also had an intellectual depth and a width of interests which were evident to those who met him and which would require expression. At Oxford, to which he went from Glasgow, the university magazine chose him as one of its *Isis* idols with the comment: 'We know of no man who has had more success, or deserved it better. He is as popular with men as he is with Fortune.' The same article contained two other interesting statements: 'He dislikes dancing, and hates ladies', and 'he refuses to be classified as a literary man'.

History and biography, the law, politics and public administration all brought him satisfaction in different ways, and by the time he was launched on his career as a thriller writer he knew enough about the exercise of power and about those who did the exercising to treat the subject with authority. This was among the reasons why he was able to steer a continuously entertaining path between the cool realism of Somerset Maugham's tales of espionage with Ashenden and the grotesque world of international intrigue in which Sexton Blake, Nayland Smith and Bulldog Drummond operate.

Buchan's heroes are successful men who enjoy the company of successful men. Richard Usborne wrote that to qualify as heroes in Buchan's works men had to merit at least a column in *The Times* when they died. The preoccupation with success is sometimes oppressive, not least because the successes themselves ring so true. We really believe that Edward Leithen, who became Attorney-

General at forty-six, won the mile at Eton. A similar claim made by or for a P.C. Wren hero makes us want to consult the record books.

Sharing, as they do, the common factor of success, the heroic figures of Buchan's thrillers tend to belong to one of two categories. Either they are romantic aristocrats, or they have qualified for a small élite group, within which they represent the different members of an English-speaking brotherhood of nations. The aristocrats include Sandy Arbuthnot, second son of the 15th Baron Clanroyden, who was educated at Eton and New College, Oxford. 'In the caravanserais of Bokhara he is known, and there are shikaris in the Pamirs who still speak of him round their fires.' On returning to England and taking part in a meeting of 'clean, hard, decent fellows', Sandy 'sat there with his merry brown face, looking absurdly young and girlish, so that the most suspicious could have seen nothing more in him than the ordinary mad English-man who lived for adventure and novelty'. Elsewhere Sandy is described as 'abstemious as a Moslem'. Supporting Sandy in the aristocratic cast is Sir Archibald (Archie) Roylance, an intrepid airman. When Richard Hannay, during an inter-war period, wants him to fly on a mission to Norway and asks him whether he is engaged for the next fortnight, Archie mentions that 'he had thought of getting back to Scotland to watch a pair of nesting greenshanks'.

Among the heroes from overseas there is Peter Pienaar, the Afrikaaner, who has two careers of distinction in the 1914-18 war, as secret agent and as airman. Sandy Arbuthnot says to him: '"You're the bravest man I ever met, and I've seen a few."' There is also the American John S. Blenkiron, whom Hannay describes as 'the best companion God ever made'. Blenkiron, who is a profes-sional intelligence man, is afflicted with a duodenal ulcer, as Buchan himself was. ' "What's life anyhow?" ' Blenkiron asks. ' "For me it's living on a strict diet and having frequent pains in my stomach." ' From this he concludes that it is not a great sacrifice to give life up ' "provided you get a good price on the deal" '. At the centre of all is Richard Hannay, who grows in stature and wordly distinction as the books succeed each other.

When we first meet Hannay in *The Thirty-Nine Steps* he is lonely and unknown. The 'pile' he has made is 'not one of the big ones, but good enough', and his main complaint is that he has 'no real pal to go about with'. He is then thirty-seven. Before very long he will have plenty of pals among the knights at the Buchan round table.

Hannay was said to have been modelled on Field-Marshal Lord Ironside, but the resemblance was probably fairly superficial. Much more decidedly he is Buchan's concept of what a hero of a thriller ought to be. He differs from Buchan in a number of important respects, particularly in his relative philistinism. When Sandy Arbuthnot asks him if he has heard of 'a thing called the superman' he replies, ' "I gather it was invented by a sportsman named Nietzsche." ' Hannay also insists on presenting himself as a rather ordinary being. When Dominick Medina in *The Three Hostages* tries to hypnotize him he attributes his ability to resist to ' "the intractable bedrock of commonplaceness in me" '. There is too something clearly at variance with Buchan's middle-class Scottish background in Hannay's statement that

> 'a man of my sort, who has travelled about the world in rough places, gets on perfectly well with two classes, what you may call the upper and the lower. . . . I was at home with herds and tramps and roadmen. . . . I was sufficiently at my ease with people like Sir Walter. . . . What fellows like me don't understand is the great comfortable, satisfied middle-class world, the folk that live in villas and suburbs.'

Hannay shares Buchan's delight in climbing and in country lore and, particularly, his consciousness of what Newbolt called 'the brotherhood that binds the brave of all the earth'. When Hannay and Peter Pienaar in *Greenmantle* carry out their dangerous mission in wartime Germany disguised as two disgruntled Dutch South Africans, they are continually meeting Germans they respect (in contrast with the perverted Colonel Stumm, who is 'an incarnation of all that makes Germany detested'). One such is the engineer Gaudian, who reappears in *The Three Hostages,* by which time he has been transferred to the side the reader supports. Hannay's judgment on him is: ' "Gaudian was clearly a good fellow, a white man and a gentleman. I could have worked with him, for he belonged to my totem." ' Then there is Captain Zorn. ' "That fellow gave me the best 'feel' of any German I had yet met. He was a white man and I could have worked with him. I liked his stiff chin and steady blue eyes." ' 'White man' as a term of approbation occurs fairly frequently. During a period of comparative inaction in Turkey Hannay has a ride, and the exercise causes him to feel 'more like a white man'. Blenkiron falls into the habit too and describes Julius Victor as 'the whitest Jew since the Apostle Paul'. And when Peter Pienaar, who has become disillusioned with Europe, says ' "there is only one white man's land, and that is South Africa" ', his words do not have quite the meaning that would be attributed to them today.

In *The Thirty-Nine Steps* Buchan found he could do without a heroine of any kind. Indeed there are only two women in the book, a 'decent old body' who gives Hannay a bowl of milk with whisky when he is on the run, and another who makes a brief appearance in the train on his journey north. Hollywood script-writers did of course subsequently make good the omission. In *Greenmantle* there is the slightly absurd adventuress, Hilda von Einem. When Hannay encounters her he states: 'Women had never come much my way, and I knew about as much of their ways as I knew about the Chinese language.' Shortly afterwards he admits: 'I had never been in a motor car with a lady before, and I felt like a fish on a dry sandbank.' He was, it should be remembered, thirty-seven in the earlier book. In *Mr Standfast* Mary Lamington appears, and as soon as she does so we know we can look forward to the prospect of matrimony. Yet even she is barely presented as a woman.

She seemed little more than a child. . . . A figure kept going and coming—a young girl with a cloud of gold hair, and the strong, slim grace of a boy, who had sung 'Cherry Ripe' in a moonlit garden. . . . She kissed me gravely like a wise child.

In fact Mary Lamington is not only grown up enough to be a V.A.D.; she is also something in the secret service, something, of course, pretty successful.

In a letter to his sister, herself a distinguished novelist, who wrote under the name O. Douglas, Buchan wrote: 'You draw a wonderful picture of a woman (a thing I could about as much do as fly to the moon.)' He was not far wrong. A Buchan heroine is likely to be distinguished by her enthusiasm for beagling as by anything else, and Richard Usborne spotted that one of them, Janet Raden, who married Archie Roylance, was not only a good walker but 'famous for her wind'. In general Buchan was probably not much interested in women. In her biography of him Janet Adam Smith quotes a childhood friend, who said of Buchan and his sister: 'John and Anna didn't have love affairs'. There was probably too an element of prudery in his make-up. Recalling an occasion when he and Henry James had examined some documents concerning Lady Byron, he wrote that whereas James had not turned a hair, he himself was 'nearly made sick' by the 'ancient indecency'. But stronger than indifference or prudery were the qualities of reticence and fidelity. When Buchan wrote, after proposing to his future wife, 'you are the only woman I have ever been in love with, and shall ever be in love with', he was almost certainly expressing and forecasting the truth. He seems to have had a supremely happy marriage, which was yet another great achievement. In contrast with this it is perhaps of little importance that the way in which life is ordained in the Buchan world seems a little hard on Hilda von Einem, let alone the girl who was famous for her wind.

In one respect at least Richard Hannay—and here he can safely be identified with Buchan—was Newbolt Man in his purest form. Three separate missions are carried out in enemy territory in *Greenmantle*: one by Sandy Arbuthnot, the artist in disguises; one by Blenkiron, the professional; and one by Hannay assisted by Peter Pienaar. Blenkiron complains that he seems to have achieved nothing, and Hannay comments: 'I was mean enough to feel rather glad. He had been the professional with the best chance. It would be a good joke if the amateur succeeded where the professional failed.' Amateur status was a necessary qualification for captaincy when Buchan was writing, as it was for many years afterwards, and Hannay was a natural captain. Indeed, if the Newbolt Man club were to field a celestial eleven, it would, I am inclined to think, be General Sir Richard Hannay who would lead them out from the pavilion. He would not be the most brilliant performer; as he did not get into the team until he was thirty–seven he would not be the sprightliest in the field; but he would have studied the other side's weaknesses, he would know when to change the bowling, and he would ensure—not that it would be necessary—exemplary conduct from everyone who played under his captaincy.

The series of books telling the adventures of Richard Hannay may reasonably be regarded as the culmination of a process whereby Newbolt Man developed from Victorian schoolboy to twentieth–century secret agent, from Elizabethan sailor to World War I general. New heroes in the familiar stamp would continue to be created, but while Buchan was writing forces were already gathering strength which would soon undermine the foundations of the social philosophy to which Hannay and his associates subscribed and shake the social order in which they were nurtured. Among these was a sudden revival of an old literary and social tradition, the tradition of Robin Hood and even of Dick Turpin. By the turn of the century this had already emerged in a new and startling embodiment, that of A.J.Raffles, burglar and county cricketer.

The original title of the book in which Raffles first confronted his public was *The Amateur Cracksman*. His amateur status, both as cricketer and burglar, is Raffles's principal source of pride. He is 'a dangerous bat, a brilliant field, and perhaps the very finest slow bowler of his decade', yet cricket to him is a pastime. He does, it is true, have a little net practice before the first match of the season, but for this he places sovereigns instead of bails on the stumps, a sovereign being tossed to any professional who bowls him. When he is invited to Lord Amersteth's country home because of his cricketing skill he feels insulted. ' "Nothing," ' he says, ' "riles me more than being asked about for my cricket as though I were a pro. myself." ' During this visit he and a professional burglar both plan to steal Lady Melrose's diamonds, and the contest between them strikes Raffles as being like 'Gentlemen and Players at single wicket'.

The public-school background is also important in Raffles's development. The narrator, Bunny, who is unable to pay his gambling debts and has issued some dud cheques in consequence, turns to Raffles for help because Raffles, when captain of the eleven, had been kind to him at school. ' "Everybody knows," ' Bunny declares, ' "how largely the tone of a public school depends on that of the eleven, and on the character of the captain of cricket in particular; and I have never heard it denied that in A.J. Raffles's time our tone was good." ' This was in spite of the fact that Raffles was in the habit of patrolling the town at night in loud checks and a false beard.

Bunny finds Raffles 'beyond comparison' the most masterful man he has ever known, and he writes of 'his indolent, athletic figure; his pale, sharp, clean-shaven features; his curly black hair'. But Raffles also has a 'strong unscrupulous mouth'. He and Bunny are described as living the lives of 'hundreds of other young fellows about town'—i.e. doing no work—but their 'game' or 'sport' is burglary. They have their scruples, and Raffles at least is capable of magnanimous gestures, but, unlike Robin Hood, they steal in the main to enrich themselves. Raffles even uses an Australian girl, who is attracted to him, as an unwitting assistant in an attempt to steal a diamond. Bunny at this point refers to Raffles's 'experience of women (a side of his character upon which I have never previously touched, for it deserves another volume).'

E.W. Hornung, the creator of Raffles, was Conan Doyle's brother–in–law, and when the concept of Raffles was first explained to him Doyle was shocked. He told Hornung sternly that he must not make a criminal a hero. Some years later M.R. Ridley wrote that 'in 1899 *Raffles, the Amateur Cracksman* hit the late Victorian public with a crashing broadside between wind and water, and the hero . . . became something of a household word'. In his second book devoted to Raffles's exploits, *The Black Mask,* Hornung was more circumspect. Raffles is now a much less glamorous character, furtively concealing his identity from virtually everyone except Bunny. 'Raffles was a genius, and he could not make it pay! . . . Altogether it was a very different story from the old, unsuspected club and cricket days, with their *noctes ambrosianae* at the Albany.' The end for Raffles was to be killed in the South African war. It was an appropriate one, for he could not have survived as A.J. Raffles the cricketer. Yet his spirit lived on in a manner which would have shocked and surprised Ballantyne and Reed, Henty and Haggard, for it manifested itself in characters whose social backgrounds were similar to those of many of their own heroes.

Edgar Wallace devised one such character known both as Anthony and the Avenger, who dispenses his own interpretation of justice. ' "I am a public benefactor." ' he claims in *The Mixer.* ' "I confine my depredations to the crooks." ' He has two assistants named Paul and Sandy, and they all have military decorations ' "which we would scorn to mention in view of our present nefarious employment" '. Paul even has the distinction of being an officer of the League (*sic*) of Honour. Anthony wears immaculate evening dress and fights according to the Queensberry rules and other sporting codes. 'Anthony's fist caught him under the jaw. . . . Anthony had low–tackled his assailant.' Inevitably, it seems, his victims are people with names such as Burnstid and Leggenstein, who are respectively 'a very stout man, with a large, healthy face, and a large, healthy nose', who is 'always well–

dressed and even better than that', and 'a tall, lithe, dark young man, rather flashily dressed', who wears 'diamond rings on his well–manicured hands'. (How, it seems reasonable to ask, did Jewish readers react to Edgar Wallace's enormous popularity?)

Perhaps the most famous of all modern English criminal heroes is one who came into being between the two world wars and who survived long beyond the second, undergoing in the course of his career a successful transplantation from Britain to the United States, from book covers to cinema and television screens. This is Leslie Charteris's Simon Templar or the Saint. By 1956 Simon Templar is able to say of himself:

> 'I never robbed anyone who wasn't a thief or a blackguard, although they might have been clever enough to stay within the law. I've killed people too, but never anyone the world wasn't a better place without. Sometimes people seem to forget it, since I got to be too well known and had to give up some of the simple methods I used to get away with when I was more anonymous, but my name used to stand for a kind of justice, and I haven't changed.'

Simon Templar may not have changed, but others have, particularly girls, who can now confidently be described as having figures 'of noteworthy exuberance in the upper register'.

The revival of the Robin Hood tradition was not a powerful protest against the existing social order. It was perhaps more the expression of a feeling that a social order, which had been thoroughly satisfactory, was changing for the worse because money and power were passing into the wrong hands. A much more cogent cause of the ultimate demise of Newbolt Man, and of the destruction of so much of what he stood for, was the discovery by certain writers of what war and patriotism could mean in practice. These were writers who spent much of the war of 1914-18 in the trenches, an experience which Buchan and Newbolt, for example, were spared. Yet even among those who had fought in the trenches there were some who not only continued to present Newbolt Man in fiction, but who extolled his virtues with a new, though sometimes frenzied, fervour.

The authors whose clubland heroes Richard Usborne examined together with those of Buchan were Dornford Yates and Sapper, both pseudonymous writers. Jonah Mansel, the creation of Dornford Yates, is in the established tradition of Newbolt Man, even to the point of being able to say: 'I'm no good at women.' But Jonah, when he is engaged in international adventure and espionage, seems to me on temporary loan from the world of Dornford Yates's *Berry & Co.,* and this world is in itself a *cri–de–coeur* from an author who already in 1919 seemed to fear that society was no longer ordered as it should be. This weakness he attempted to repair by creating a world of his own, in which it was manifestly right that those who had inherited wealth, i.e. Berry & Co., should spend it as they chose, just as it was manifestly wrong that those who had acquired wealth, i.e. Messrs Lewis, Dunkelsbaum and Bladder, should spend it as *they* chose. Berry & Co. can normally be relied on to win, and in practice they suffer little inconvenience beyond what may be caused by a laundry strike, the vagaries of a temporary cook and a seemingly endless succession of flat tyres. The level of income tax and servants' wages *circa* 1920 gives them some cause for concern, but the Sealyham dog, which has an unerring instinct for distinguishing between a Dunkelsbaum and a family friend, can still be rewarded with a caviar sandwich.

Bulldog Drummond, Sapper's most famous character, is by contrast almost a creation of the trenches. When he first appears in the book which bears his name he is quite an engaging young man. He whistles cheerfully in his bath while his needs are attended to by James Denny, his 'square–jawed ex–batman', and 'that excellent woman', Mrs Denny, who grills bacon and kidneys 'to a turn'. Drummond has placed an advertisement in a newspaper stating: 'Demobilised officer, finding peace increasingly tedious, would welcome diversion.' This leads him to meet Phyllis, his future wife, whom he finds an adorable girl. Adorable girls, we are told, are a hobby of his, and in next to no time he is calling Phyllis 'old thing'.

Drummond is a convincing combination of athlete and philistine. His nose was damaged in the final of the public schools heavyweight boxing championship; he is 'no judge of art', his knowledge of French is 'microscopic', and 'like most normal Englishmen, politics and labour disputes had left him cold'. To his creator he is 'a sportsman and a gentlemen. And the combination of the two is an unbeatable production'. Nor is there any reason to doubt the powers of leadership which he exercises over his friends: Peter Darrell, who in spite of coming home with the milk every morning turns out for Middlesex at cricket, and Algy Longworth, who wears an entirely unnecessary eye–glass but who 'under a cloak of assumed flippancy . . . concealed an iron nerve which had never yet failed him'. Denny of course and, indeed, Mrs Denny accept danger as part of their terms of employment. The story races along at speed, and there is a certain consistency within the general implausibility. Yet already in this first volume there are isolated sentences suggesting that all is not well in post–war Britain.

Jerome K. Green, an American detective, says to Drummond: ' "Your little old country, Captain, is, saving one, the finest on God's earth; but she's in a funny mood. She's sick, like most of us are; maybe she's a little bit sicker than a good many people think." ' Drummond himself, in spite of his lack of interest in politics, finds 'odd things' recurring to him: 'trade unions refusing to allow discharged soldiers to join them; the reiterated threats of direct action'. It is also perhaps significant that Peter Darrell foresees no difficulty in rounding up 'at least fifty demobilised soldiers who are on for a scrap'. But Drummond himself in this book is concerned with little except Phyllis and what he regards as a sporting contest with the arch–villain, Carl Petersen, and Petersen presents no more serious a threat to society as it is, or ever has been, than does Fu–Manchu.

In *The Black Mask* a great deal has changed. Drummond is already a well-known figure among readers, and, as with Hannay, although in a much more sinister manner, this seems to have raised his status in his own world. He has even progressed from a two-seater—just the thing for courting Phyllis—to a Rolls-Royce, and he is now engaged politically in his own form of direct action.

The events take place in the early 1920s, yet the very title of the book may be considered prophetic, for Drummond and his followers—the term 'followers' is now more appropriate than 'friends'—dress up in black and violently assault those whom for political, racial or other reasons they dislike. Moreover their violence is not only punitive but something which they actively enjoy.

Drummond, now referred to as 'the leader', has discovered a gang of Bolshevik conspirators.

> 'Good,' said the leader. 'Let us continue the inspection. What are these two Hebrews?'
>
> A man from behind stepped forward and examined them slowly; then he came up to the leader and whispered in his ear.
>
> 'Is that so?' A new and terrible note had crept into the deep voice. 'My friends and I do not like your trade, you swine. It is well that we have come provided with the necessary implement for such a case. Fetch the cat.'

After the Jews have 'flung themselves grovelling on the floor, screaming for mercy', we learn that they have managed, somewhat unusually, to combine the occupations of Bolshevik conspirator and white-slave trader.

Not long after this Drummond drives a Member of Parliament to permanent lunacy by visiting him in his bedroom and informing him that he has lit a fuse and a guncotton explosion will follow shortly. Then there is Count Zadowa, who is a hunchback. 'It jarred on Drummond to fight him as if he had been a normal man. So he flogged him with a rhinoceros whip till his arm ached.'

There is still a pretence that the gang consists of nice, athletic, indolent men-about-town. Inspector McIver of Scotland Yard, for instance, who may be thought remarkably obtuse in not having discovered that Drummond and his friends are the Black Gang, and correspondingly remiss in not having preferred the appropriate charges, retains a deep-seated respect for them.

> A strange caste, he reflected, as he sipped his drink; a caste which does not aim at, because it essentially is, good form; a caste which knows only one fetish—the absolute repression of all visible emotion; a caste which incidentally pulled considerably more than its own weight in the war. McIver gave them credit for that.

Drummond too retains certain rather preposterous moral scruples, which derive from his understanding of sport. Having already acquired a fairly extensive homicidal record, he finds himself fighting for his life and knowing that while he does so Phyllis is at the mercy of Petersen's gang. His antagonist is about to throttle him when Drummond suddenly remembers he has a clasp-knife. 'It went against his grain to use it; never before had he fought an unarmed man with a weapon.' He does in fact use the knife, but only in order to force the other man to let go his grip. He then kills him with his bare hands in accordance with the precepts of his Japanese instructor.

Through the other volumes in the series Drummond battles on, still clinging pathetically to his war-time rank, whereas Peter Darrell, Algy Longworth and the others have long since reverted to the more dignified 'Mr'. He is still accepted as a leader. The narrator of *The Final Count,* John Stockton, who is a barrister, states: 'In the Army I never took kindly to discipline. And yet when Drummond gave an order I never questioned, I never hesitated.' He is still presented as a huge man, and this in itself seems odd by modern standards, for we learn that in reality he 'stood just six feet in his socks, and turned the scale at over fourteen stone.' If he were to aspire to be a lock forward in high-grade rugby football today, the commentators would probably refer to his lack of weight and inches, and the breezier ones might even call him 'little Drummond'. But as his contests with Petersen become increasingly bizarre and the two men's admiration for each other grows, we are more and more aware that Drummond has long since ceased to be the engaging young man whose newspaper advertisement brought him into contact with Phyllis.

The name Sapper gave to the genus of human being whom he admired unreservedly was 'the Breed'. Of a member of the Breed, Derek Vane, he wrote in *Mufti*:

> On matters connected with literature, or art, or music, his knowledge was microscopic. Moreover, he regarded with suspicion anyone who talked intelligently on such subjects. On the other hand he had been in the eleven at Eton, and was a scratch golfer. He had a fine seat on a horse and rode straight; he could play a passable game of polo, and was a good shot.

Sapper was fully aware that the Breed had taken a bad knock, though he had no doubts about its survival.

> They are always the same, and they are branded with the stamp of the Breed. They shake your hand as a man shakes it; they meet your eye as a man meets it. Just now a generation of them lies around Ypres and La Bassée. . . . Dead, yes; but not the Breed. The Breed never dies.

In Bulldog Drummond Sapper created a member of the Breed who survived the slaughter but who was, in his way, a delayed casualty of the 1914-18 war, just as, in their different ways, were Adolf Hitler, Hermann Goering and Rudolf Hess. The books recounting Drummond's contests with Carl Petersen may have lost some of their impact as thrillers, but they still provide an interesting case-history of the onset and development of a not uncommon neurotic condition in a once quite likable and generous young man.

That young man, slowly ageing, occupied a leading position in English popular fiction for about a decade. It was approximately the decade which elapsed between the return of the demobilized soldiers and the delayed but devastating emergence of a new school of serious writing. The quality linking members of this school was a determination to describe war in a manner in which it had never yet been presented to readers of English popular fiction.

CHAPTER EIGHT

The Aftermath of War

R.C. Sherriff's *Journey's End* was produced at the Savoy Theatre in London in January 1929 after being tried out by the Incorporated Stage Society a month earlier. A number of managements had declined to handle *Journey's End*, no doubt in the belief that audiences were unlikely to be attracted to a play in which the action takes place in a rat–infested dug–out fifty yards from the front line; in which the hero and company commander, who is twenty–one, is drinking a bottle of whisky a day to steady his nerves; in which the end, the journey's end, is the bursting of a shell on the roof of the dug–out, where a young subaltern fresh from school is lying gravely wounded; and in which, in defiance of the theatrical conventions of the time, the action is performed by an all–male cast.

Theatrical entertainment with a jingoist message had ceased to be in vogue for some time when *Journey's End* was produced, but the gap had been filled by a tendency to concentrate on what was called the lighter side of war. A safe formula for success had been a frolic featuring a comic Cockney batman and a red–faced, red–tabbed general who was not such a fire–eater as he looked, with one or two pretty little V.A.D.s popping up from time to time in unexpected places not far from the front line. *Journey's End* was something new. James Agate, the most widely quoted dramatic critic of the time, described it as 'a work of extraordinary quality and interest'. Men who had survived the trenches went to the Savoy Theatre and agreed that this was how life had been, and those who knew only the official propaganda picture of trench warfare had the thrill of a new experience. The play ran for 594 consecutive performances.

The year 1929 also saw the publication in England of Richard Aldington's *Death of a Hero* and in Germany of Erich Maria Remarque's *Im Westen nichts Neues*. The next year Remarque's book appeared in English under the title *All Quiet on the Western Front* and Siegfried Sassoon's second autobiographical work, *Memoirs of an Infantry Officer,* was published. Within a couple of years something of a revolution in the literary treatment of war had occurred, and there were some startling consequences. Pacifism became fashionable among large numbers of the literary–minded young once Beverley Nichols had written a best–seller on the subject, *Cry Havoc,* and members of the Oxford Union proclaimed by a majority vote that they would not fight for king and country.

War was a sphere of activity in which Newbolt Man was expected to shine, and war was now being presented in a new and disturbing light. But neither *Journey's End* nor *Memoirs of an Infantry Officer* did any serious damage to the conventional picture of a hero. Stanhope, the twenty-one-year-old company commander in *Journey's End,* may be in the process of becoming an alcoholic (if he survives) but he is still an officer who thinks first of his men and to whom those who serve under him are devoted. Osborne, Stanhope's relatively middle-aged second-in-command, who is known as 'Uncle', declares that he would 'go to hell with him'. From Raleigh, the newly joined subaltern, who was Stanhope's junior and hero–worshipper at school, we learn that Stanhope had been 'skipper of rugger at Barford and kept wicket for the eleven'. (Osborne did even better and played rugby football for England. ' "I was awfully lucky to get the chance. It's a long time ago now." ') When Hibbert, another of Stanhope's officers, loses his nerve badly, Stanhope explains: ' "They all feel like you do—in their hearts—and just go on sticking it because they know it's—it's the only thing a decent man can do." ' Hibbert, significantly, has a collection of dirty post-cards, which he has brought with him into the dug-out. Stanhope pretends to be amused by them, but only in order to conceal the emotions he feels on learning that Osborne has been killed.

Memoirs of an Infantry Officer is the successor to *Memoirs of a Fox-Hunting Man,* and the autobiographical character in both, who is given the name George Sherston, is a lover of cricket and the English countryside, who has the good fortune to enjoy independent means. For all his modesty he emerges as an extremely brave officer. ('Being in an exploring frame of mind, I took a bag of bombs.' . . . The battalion commander 'spoke kindly to me in his rough way, and in doing so made me very thankful that I had done what I could to tidy up the mess in No Man's Land.') Sherston makes no claim to be an intellectual and admits he is out of his depth when confronted by those at home who agree with the standpoint he eventually takes in opposing the war, but who do so on political or philosophical grounds. 'Armageddon was too immense for my solitary understanding.' But the characterization in Sassoon's memoirs is both deeper and subtler than that in *Journey's End,* and this is most apparent in the development of Sherston himself. With his sense of a spiritual union linking those who shared the experiences of the trenches, his restrained analyses of the quality of courage, his sensitivity, the love for his fellowmen which shines through his disgust at the cant of prelates and politicians and the rapaciousness of profiteers, Sherston has the qualities of a true poet. As a poet indeed Sassoon wrote about war with much more bitterness than is to be found in his autobiographical works. ('Does is matter?—losing your sight? . . . There's such splendid work for the blind.') But with all this bitterness he did little to destroy belief in the better of the ideals which inspired Newbolt Man. At most he gently undermined them. The sledgehammer work of destruction was carried out by Richard Aldington.

Aldington began to write the work which, with an irony comparable with that of Sherriff and Remarque in their choice of titles, he called *Death of a Hero,* shortly after the armistice of 1918. He soon decided that it was premature to write a book of this kind, and he did not resume work on it until ten years later. The hero of the book, George Winterbourne, ends as a captain in the Royal Foddershire Regiment. He is a painter, and a few days before the armistice he deliberately courts death from enemy action, largely because he can see no place for himself in the post–war world outside the trenches.

George Winterbourne's background is English middle–class, 'that dreadful squat pillar of the nation', which will 'only tolerate art and literature that are fifty years out of date, eviscerated, detesticulated, bowdlerised, humbuggered, subject to their anglicised Jehovah'. He belongs, we are told, to 'a nation of Mariners and Sportsmen', who 'naturally excel in the twin arts of leaving a sinking ship and kicking a man when he is down'. His headmaster extols the merits of Kipling's *If* and of the Officers Training Corps and prays that God will turn Winterbourne himself into a 'manly fellow'. Most of Winterbourne's schoolfellows accept a good deal of their headmaster's philosophy. They

> wanted to be approved and be healthy barbarians, cultivating a little smut on the sly, and finally dropping into some convenient post in life where the 'thoroughly manly fellow' was appreciated—mostly, one must admit, minor and unpleasant and not very remunerative posts in unhealthy colonies.

Winterbourne has a wife and a mistress, who enjoy each other's company and who both have 'that rather hard efficiency of the war and post–war female, veiling the ancient predatory and possessive instincts under a skilful smoke–barrage of Freudian and Havelock Ellis theories'. They find that the war, with its dying and wounded and mud and blood, all kept at a safe distance, has a strongly erotic effect on both of them. From time to time Aldington interrupts the narrative to refer to such phenomena as the latent homosexuality that lurks in so many Englishmen, causing them to be continually dissatisfied with their women, or to ask how many patriotic English gentlemen joined the Army to escape from their wives rather than to seek their country's enemies. France is presented as a much more highly civilized country than Britain, and Winterbourne finds that the horrors of war include not only fighting the Germans but living under the British.

All this is a scathing indictment of the values and standards accepted by the overwhelming majority of British officers when war broke out in 1914, and by a great many of them when it ended more than four years later. But Aldington's' most devastating blows are aimed at the conventional picture of the hero, who appears in caricature form in two of the minor figures in the book. One is even given the name of Sam Browne and is among the numerous lovers whom Winterbourne's mother takes to console herself both before and after the death of her husband. Sam Browne is 'one of those nice, clean, sporting Englishmen with a minimum of intelligence and an infinite capacity for being gulled by females, especially the clean English sort'. He is 'an adult Boy Scout, a Public School fag in shining armour—the armour of obtuseness. He met every situation in life with a formula'.

Then there is Evans, the officer whom Winterbourne, while he is still in the ranks, serves as a runner. Evans accepts every English middle-class prejudice and taboo. He is contemptuous of foreigners, disapproves of something called 'society', which he considers 'fast', has been taught to respect all women as he would his mother, played stand-off half for his school, and won his colours at cricket.

> Evans possessed that British rhinoceros equipment of min-gled ignorance, self-confidence, and complacency which is triple-armed against all the shafts of the mind. And yet Winterbourne could not help liking the man. He was exasperatingly stupid, but he was honest, he was kindly, he was conscientious, he could obey orders and command obedience in others, he took

pains to look after his men. He could be implicitly relied upon to maintain a desperate defence to the very end. There were thousands and tens of thousands like him.

For all its bitterness *Death of a Hero* enjoyed wide popularity and was published in a number of editions, including paperbacks. Its very success was an indication of how far Newbolt Man had moved from automatic acceptance as a hero, at least in certain circles, and the assault on the values he upheld was to continue in a variety of literary forms in the inter–war years.

Glorification of empire was found to be as acceptable and as easy a subject for demolition as glorification of war. Somerset Maugham, without ostensibly concerning himself with the merits or defects of the colonial system, showed, with the convincing skill of a master of narrative, how the lives of those men and women who occupied the outposts of empire could be degraded and destroyed by bitterness, disillusion and the demands of sex. George Orwell, who was more concerned with social philosophy and less with individual psychology than Maugham, wrote in *Shooting an Elephant*:

> When the white man turns tyrant it is his own freedom that he destroys. He becomes a sort of hollow, posing dummy, the conventionalized figure of a sahib. For it is a condition of his rule that he shall spend his life in trying to impress the 'natives', and so in every crisis he has got to do what the 'natives' expect of him. . . . My whole life, every white man's life in the East, was one long struggle not to be laughed at.

So he needlessly shot an elephant. When Noël Coward, with his exquisite sense of timing and rhyming, wrote that 'mad dogs and Englishmen go out in the midday sun', he seemed suddenly to have condensed the business of empire into a single sentence. After that 'pukka', 'memsahib' and 'tiffin' were among the joke–words most commonly used by the sophisticated young.

The Army as an institution continued to attract something of the obloquy directed at the war which it had fought with so much gallantry and so much mismanagement. Of all those who poured ridicule on the officer caste—and there were plenty who did—none enjoyed greater celebrity than the cartoonist, David Low. Low, who came to London from Sydney, joined the staff of the *Evening Standard* in 1927. Within a few years he had begun, through his most famous cartoon character, Colonel Blimp, to exert a political influence which extended far beyond even the considerable readership of the *Evening Standard*. Blimp became a symbol of rigidity, orthodoxy, obstinacy and obtuseness. He was not intrinsically evil himself; indeed he could at a stretch be described as a 'dear old boy'. But he was led, partly through his upbringing and caste loyalty, mainly by his lack of imagination, to support a variety of evil causes, the most dangerous of which were of course the dictatorships of Hitler and Mussolini. Blimp's prefatory 'Gad, sir', which he himself frequently uttered in a Turkish bath, was on the lips of thousands when they chose to express a deliberate absurdity, and even today liberal-minded men, when they attempt to defend some of the standards which Newbolt Man upheld, are liable to begin by saying: 'I don't want to sound like a Blimp.'

The Royal Navy has traditionally been portrayed with greater reverence by English writers than has the Army, but a new treatment was administered in the inter-war years to naval officers too, even by such a thorough and admiring student of naval history as C. S. Forester. Forester's *Brown on Resolution* was another of the books which appeared in 1929. It is no indictment of war. Indeed it is largely the account of an extremely gallant single-handed action by a naval rating which leads to the destruction of a German cruiser. But it is the naval rating, Albert Brown, who is the hero, and not Lieutenant-Commander, later Captain, R.E.S. Savill-Samarez, who, though neither of them is aware of the relationship, is Albert Brown's father. Savill-Samarez appears early in the book as 'a naval officer of the best brand of British stupidity'. To Agatha Brown, by whom he has an illegitimate son, he is 'a

man whom one only loved as one might love a pet St Bernard'.
When he is in command of H.M.S. *Leopard* we are told that

> he was never a man for deep thought or of much imagination.
> . . . Little jobs like picking up moorings in a twenty–thousand-
> ton battleship in a crowded harbour with a full gale blowing he
> had simply accepted and carried through with automatically-
> acquired skill, and without any frightening pictures of what
> might happen if he made a mistake.

When he thinks he may be able to sink the German cruiser
as a consequence of the efforts of his illegitimate son, of which
he knows nothing, he reflects that 'it would be very handy if he
went in for politics; it might bring him a K.C.B.' This in turn
might 'obtain for him a fat, comfortable colonial governorship on
his retirement'. Rider Haggard's Captain Good did not think like
that, or if he did we were not informed of it.

Institutional loyalties, in particular the one which had meant
so much through the years to Newbolt Man, loyalty to the public
school, also became ready targets for ridicule. Among the most
popular entertainers in cabaret and on radio in Britain in the 1930s
were two cousins who called themselves the Western Brothers, and
who sang songs which George Western accompanied on the piano.
Their fame was based almost entirely on two catch–lines. One
was 'Play the game, you cads'. The other was 'Wearing his old
school tie'. Their appeal was exclusively to audiences of a period.
When George Western died in 1969 he had for some years spent
his working hours in charge of a sweet and tobacco kiosk at Wey-
bridge station.

The emergence of a new and, by conventional standards, un-
heroic kind of hero, the little man baffled by the complexity of
modern life, was another phenomenon of the inter–war years. The
most famous specimen was the screen character of Charles Chaplin,
but he was by no means unique. In an article which he wrote for
the *Strand* magazine Winston Churchill commented on the significance of the contrast between the little man with the forlorn

features created by Strube, the *Daily Express* cartoonist, and the traditional figure of John Bull 'with his big stick and resolute, rugged face'.

Indeed, of the ideals which inspired Newbolt Man the one which came nearest to passing unscathed through the 1930s was probably amateurism. Excellent cricket matches continued to be played between the Gentlemen and the Players, and if around 1930 an opinion poll had been conducted among those interested in cricket, it is possible that a majority would have expressed the hope that the Gentlemen would win. It was only after 1945, when British managerial talent in industry was thought to compare unfavourably with that of other nations, and the British began to be defeated repeatedly at games which they had invented by competitors from the most surprising countries, that the moral ascendancy of the amateur over the professional was seriously disputed.

Those writers whom regular readers of popular fiction were most likely to respect as masters of the serious novel did little too in the inter-war years to promote the cult of the heroic. John Galsworthy allowed the blood of the Forsytes to run pretty thin after 1918: Jon Forsyte is a nice boy and a good son to his mother, but he is not cast in the heroic mould. Wells never again gave his readers characters as memorable as those of his pre-1914 novels. Bennett as early as 1911 had created in Denry Machin a hero-type whose talents were directed towards the surprising object of making money. The public first warmed to J. B. Priestley because of the apparent authenticity of the provincial industrial background from which such a homely figure as Jess Oakroyd emerged. Of the novelists most esteemed by critics and literary historians, John Gross, in *The Rise and Fall of the Man of Letters*, wrote:

> In the 1920s the dominant characteristic of modern literature was felt to be a bringing to light of hidden areas of the personality, an enlarging and refining of consciousness. Joyce's interior monologues, Lawrence's insistence that 'you mustn't look in my novels for the old stable ego of the character', Virginia Woolf's flow of tremulous energy. . . .

It was a fair appraisal and one implying a pretty minor role for the man of action.

A number of the most popular novelists in the 1930s were women, some specializing in romance, some in the detective story, and women have seldom created characters bearing more than a superficial resemblance to Newbolt Man in his purest form. The detective story designed as an intellectual puzzle, with rules for its construction as severe as any by which French classical dramatists were bound—the kind of book of which Stevenson wrote that it 'remains enthralling, but insignificant, like a game of chess, not a work of human art'—probably reached its peak in the 1930s. As an alternative, perhaps as a reaction, to this rather astringent form of entertainment there was also a vogue for the tough–guy thriller, in which the central character was either an American importation or else a more or less convincing native copy of one.

With all these new fashions, new philosophies, new taboos, Newbolt Man clearly faced a struggle for survival. His spirit persisted fairly strongly for a time in writings for boys. The pupils at Greyfriars school changed neither their code of conduct nor their idiom, and the Westerman history lessons continued to exert their appeal. A contest conducted through public libraries in the 1930s showed Westerman to be the most popular boys' author in a number of towns. A new popular hero in the traditional mould even merged in the works of a prolific writer of books before, during and after the war of 1939-45. The writer was Captain W. E. Johns, a former journalist who had specialized in aviation, and the creator of Biggles. As an intrepid pilot Biggles has adventures over a wide area of the earth's surface, but it is difficult not to regard him as an anachronism, particularly when his second–in–command, who goes by the name of Algy, says: ' "If my guv'nor sees my mug in the papers he'll throw a fit" ', or when he himself says to Algy: ' "You can't go on flirting with Consuelo unless you intend marrying her." '

The war of 1939-45, differing so greatly in its conduct as it did from that of 1914-18, might have been expected to throw up new fictional characters such as Buchan could have created. Young men from leading English public schools, who had been educated at Oxford or Cambridge, did carry out missions of the kind depicted in *Greenmantle*. Others who had been parachuted into occupied territory found themselves in daily contact with leaders of partisan forces. There were long–range desert groups, private armies, commandos, as well as fighter or bomber pilots who were briefly national heroes. Such men wrote their memoirs; they did not seem to find a Buchan to translate them into fiction.

Not long after the end of the war in 1945 a new folk hero did emerge in Britain through the medium of radio. This was Dick Barton, spy–catcher and scourge of black market operators, smugglers and bullion robbers. It was estimated that on any evening between a fifth and a third of the population of Britain listened to his exploits, and great care was taken to make him a suitable hero for such a huge audience. Dick Barton was an ex–commando, he attended a grammar school, and he then went on to Glasgow University. His father, so far from owning rolling acres, was born in Sheffield and began work as an errand–boy.

Dick Barton satisfied a need in his time, but it would be difficult now to locate his spiritual successors. When men who had served in the war began to write novels based on their war service they were liable to express admiration for a quality new in the English fictional hero. This was professionalism. In Nicholas Monsarrat's highly successful *The Cruel Sea* the reader is expected to identify himself with the young officer Lockhart, who is serving for the duration of the war, but Lockhart recognizes a quality in Captain Ericson which he himself will never acquire.

> Lockhart had never admired the Captain more than during the twelve hours that followed. . . . It was the professional sense which was now the mainspring of every sustained effort of will; the feeling, present all the time, that senior officers of

escorts were specifically hired to sink U–boats and that for this reason U–boats must never be allowed to go to waste.

Naval officers could fight their battles only in time of war, but secret agents could operate perpetually, and some time after 1945 a new kind of secret agent became firmly entrenched in popular English fiction, one who was as professionally qualified as he was socially sophisticated.

He had been in many a tight corner before, and courage, quick wits, endurance, audacity, or some combination of them, had always saved him; but now . . . hundreds of tons of water forced him fathoms deep. . . . To keep his mind off Erika he tried to conjure up scenes from his life before he met her. . . . Sabine, the beautiful Hungarian, as he had first met her at the casino at Deauville; lovely, laughing Phyllis, with whom he had taken a stolen holiday up the Rhine, wicked little black–eyed Minette. . . .

This particular hero writes, by way of a preface, a letter to the author who created him, in which he states: 'I still have a little of the Pol Roger '28 you sent me in return for my last batch of notes. . . . This time I rather favour Louis Roederer '45.' No, it is not James Bond, but someone who, in Richard Hannay's phrase, is of the same totem, Dennis Wheatley's hero, Gregory Sallust.

Ian Fleming's James Bond acquired the greatest fame of any of his totem. With his professionalism, his ruthlessness, his expertise in wine, women and weaponry, Bond may reasonably be considered the antithesis of Newbolt Man in every respect except two. Both men have courage and both serve their country faithfully. But all heroes have courage, and all heroes are loyal to some cause, whether king, country or faith.

The British reading public adopted Bond as a new folk–hero, just as the listening public had earlier adopted Dick Barton. Their choice of Bond indicated how wide the gulf had become between Newbolt Man and the mass of readers. For some readers at least the gulf was soon to be widened even further with the cult of the anti-hero, for this was a being with whom Newbolt Man shared nothing except their common humanity. His life-span began only when the species *homo newboltiensis* as hero in fiction was already largely extinct.

CHAPTER NINE

Newbolt Man:
Reality and Summary

The age in which Newbolt Man flourished in fiction may be roughly defined as extending from the school days of Tom Brown to Bulldog Drummond's last encounter with Irma, 'the female of the species', Carl Petersen's accomplice. As an adult he enjoyed his greatest fictional successes before, during and shortly after the South African war. In real life, if an approximation to Newbolt Man, or even a personification of him, is to be sought, it may perhaps be found in an individual who, appropriately, first came into prominence through the siege of Mafeking. This was Robert Stephenson Smyth Baden-Powell, a man who not only launched a youth movement of world-wide appeal, but who in doing so codified the ethos of a class and a period more effectively, it may be thought, than anyone else. The ethos was largely that proclaimed in the publications of the Religious Tract Society, in particular in the first number of the *Boy's Own Paper*.

Baden-Powell had the right kind of professional middle-class background to equip him for the task to which he devoted himself in later life, his father being a Church of England parson with a large family. The success he achieved in the Army, which was considerable, was not, he insisted, due to any natural intellectual gifts. ('I was not a clever boy nor, I grieve to say, was I as industrious as I ought to have been.') He took pleasure in relating that Field–Marshal Sir Henry Wilson twice failed to pass the Army entrance examination and does not seem to have considered that this reflected in any way on the system of promotion to senior ranks in the Army.

In his autobiographical work, *Lessons from the Varsity of Life,* Baden–Powell continually emphasized the salutary influence of sport in solving personal and even political problems. 'Had the bond of sportsmanship been allowed to continue,' he wrote, 'which brought Boer and Briton together in the hunting field . . . there would today have been a close feeling of friendship, if not a fusion of the two [*sic*] races in those parts'. Instead there was 'the wretched Boer war'.

Much of the sport described consists of slaughtering animals. Hog–hunting is admitted to be a brutal sport, 'yet I loved it, as I loved the fine old fellow I fought against'. Elsewhere we read: 'Unable to gratify my lust for a hippo as a pet in an English home I have to content myself with the next best thing—the skull of one as a memento.' (If a man is prevented by the proprieties from introducing a pretty maidservant into his home, would the next best thing be to display her skull as a memento?)

'A wider conception of the Brotherhood of man' is an ideal advanced with fervour, and some of the races which qualify for inclusion in it are fairly predictable. Baden–Powell claimed to have many friends among the Bedouin, whose hospitality and sportsmanship he had enjoyed. The sad fate of a Matabele named Jan, who was killed by a lion while defending his master, a celebrated big-game hunter, is summed up with the words: 'Yes—Jan had proved himself a white man—if in a black skin.' The homelands of the élite also include, more surprisingly, Albania. 'A ripping country to shoot in. It's getting too civilised now.' Much of Baden–Powell's extensive travelling was combined with espionage, which he regarded as a particularly attractive sport, largely because of the risks which had to be run. His urge to engage in it grew on him, he declared, much as a desire for drink affects some other people.

Women play no part in Baden–Powell's reminiscences—and it may be deduced that they played little part in his life—except in such roles as wife and mother, and he did not come to know his future wife until he was in his mid–fifties. Then on board the liner *Arcadian* he admired the skill and grace she displayed in the sports. On first seeing her he had been impressed by the way she moved her feet, which, he declared, 'showed her to be possessed of honesty of purpose and common sense as well as the spirit of adventure'. If the success of the marriage which followed is any guide, this seems to have been a more satisfactory basis on which to choose a wife than most men's.

In his autobiographical work Baden–Powell cited as an ideal 'men who are acceptable at a dance and invaluable in a shipwreck', but the words were not his. His own codification of what was required of men, and of boys, came as a direct result of his experiences in the South African war. During the siege of Mafeking Lord Edward Cecil, Baden–Powell's chief staff officer, used the boys of the town to relieve the orderlies and messengers of some of their duties. Baden–Powell was so impressed by the way the boys entered into their new role that soon afterwards he began to outline a system of training based on what he had learnt. The moral purposes which this training was to serve were later defined in the famous Scout Law of ten points. These are too well known to be repeated here in full, but three of them may appropriately be quoted:

> A Scout's honour is to be trusted. . . . A Scout smiles and whistles under all difficulties. . . . A Scout is clean in thought, word and deed.

Baden–Powell understood boys well, as Ballantyne and Reed and Henty had done before him. 'The Patrol system,' he wrote, 'is merely putting your boys into permanent gangs under the leadership of one of their own number, which is their natural organization whether bent on mischief or for amusement.' This may have been a truism, but it reveals one reason for the success of the Scout movement, its founder's understanding of what could be translated into practice. Though untrained scientifically, Baden-Powell was also a gifted natural anthropologist, and he learnt and applied much from his study of the methods used by Zulus for testing a boy's fitness to accept the privileges of manhood. But the Scout movement made the appeal and impact it did, not simply because of the form of its training syllabus, but because of the ideals it propounded. These ideals were clearly British in inception and peculiarly English in their expression, yet they proved to be exportable. By the 1930s the scoutmaster, knobbly knees emphasized by the wearing of shorts, emitting unconvincing imitations of bird-cries, and wearing a hat designed for the African *veld,* was readily accepted as a figure of fun in Britain, as readily as a blimpish colonel or the wearer of an old school tie. Yet not even ridicule could hamper the world-wide spread of the movement. Some seventy years after the relief of Mafeking the number of Scouts in the world was about twelve million. The number of Girl Guides was over six million. 'I include girls,' Baden-Powell wrote, 'as well as men under the term "fellows".'

Has the world lost or gained morally by the elimination—and it seems today almost a total elimination—of Newbolt Man as a hero? It is a question not easily answered. Newbolt Man was a fighting man. He could hardly have been otherwise, given the time of his creation, for he was brought into being more or less concurrently with the Darwino–Marxist school of thought. Interpreting life and change disproportionately in terms of conflict, conflict between species, conflict between classes, this school of thought has dominated too much of human belief and far too much of human action for a century or more.

The muscular Christianity of Newbolt Man was at worst a perversion, at best a caricature of the Christian gospel. His philistinism served to widen a largely unnecessary gulf between athlete and aesthete, manliness and art, and so impoverish life. His attitude to women was a curious compound of fear and self–distrust, causing him at one moment to elevate women on to a rather chilling pedestal, at the next to regard them as a kind of permanent second eleven, one or two of whom might in an emergency be allowed to field as substitutes. His lust for slaughtering wild animals was as ecologically damaging as it was morally insensitive. His attitude towards most foreigners, and all coloured people, was never better than patronizing. In a number of ways therefore he attenuated, even degraded, the relationship between man and God, man and woman, man and man, and man and beast. Yet he had many compensating qualities.

He was loyal, personally as well as institutionally loyal. He was truthful, dependable and predictable. He served, not for profit or power or fame, though these were sometimes by–products of his actions, but for the satisfaction of service and the fulfilment of duty. His posture towards established authority was never obsequious, was deferential only when merit sanctioned it, and was generally governed by a healthy scepticism. He may have been no more than acceptable at a dance, but he was certainly invaluable in a shipwreck.

In a world of politburo and management consultancy, of nuclear fission and protest by violence, the standards to which he subscribed may be ignored, brushed aside even, as readily as is the Christian faith. But in his prime he was the idol of millions, and not only of his fellow–countrymen. True to his creed he played up and played the game. The question unresolved is whether, all things considered, his game was worth playing. In the age and in the places in which he played it I, for one, think it was.

Bibliographical Note

The principal sources I have consulted have of course been the novels and magazine stories dealt with in this book as well as their authors' autobiographies, memoirs and letters. A number of the other works to whose authors I am indebted are mentioned in the text. For convenience I am appending the following short list of secondary sources which I have found exceptionally valuable:

BIOGRAPHIES

MACK, EDWARD C., and ARMYTAGE, W.II.G., *Thomas Hughes* (Ernest Benn, 1952).

MARTIN, ROBERT BERNARD, *The Dust of Combat. A Life of Charles Kingsley* (Faber and Faber, 1959).

QUAYLE, ERIC, *Ballantyne the Brave* (Hart–Davis, 1967).

MORISON, STANLEY, *Talbot Baines Reed, Author, Bibliographer, Typefounder* (Cambridge University Press, 1960).

FENN, G. MANVILLE, *George Alfred Henty. The Story of an Active Life* (Blackie, 1907).

CARRINGTON, CHARLES, *Rudyard Kipling, His Life and Work* (Macmillan, 1955).

CONNELL, JOHN, *W.E. Henley* (Constable, 1949).

COHEN, MORTON, *Rider Haggard, His Life and Work* (Macmillan, 1968).

NORDON, PIERRE, *Conan Doyle* (John Murray, 1966).

LANE, MARGARET, *Edgar Wallace* (Hamish Hamilton, 1964).

STANDISH, ROBERT, *The Prince of Storytellers* (Peter Davies, 1957).

SMITH, JANET ADAM, *John Buchan* (Hart-Davis, 1965).

REYNOLDS, E.E., *Baden-Powell* (Oxford University Press, 1942).

WORKS OF CRITICISM

TURNER, E.S., *Boys will be Boys* (Michael Joseph, 1948).

USBORNE, RICHARD, *Clubland Heroes* (Constable, 1953).

GREENBERGER, ALLEN J., *The British Image of India. A Study in the Literature of Imperialism* (Oxford University Press, 1969).

POUND, REGINALD, *The Strand Magazine 1891–1950* (Heinemann, 1966).

ORWELL, GEORGE, *Inside the Whale and Other Essays* (Gollancz, 1940).

MURCH, A.E., *The Development of the Detective Novel* (Peter Owen, 1958).

CROUCH, MARCUS, *Treasure Seekers and Borrowers. Children's Books in Britain 1900-1960* (The Library Association, 1962).

WATSON, COLIN, *Snobbery with Violence* (Eyre and Spottiswoode, 1971).

GROSS, JOHN, *The Rise and Fall of the Man of Letters* (Weidenfeld and Nicolson, 1969).